Nowhere People

HENRY REYNOLDS is the author of fourteen books, including *An Indelible Stain?*, *The Other Side of the Frontier*, *Black Pioneers*, *Fate of a Free People*, *This Whispering in Our Hearts* and the award-winning *Why Weren't We Told?* Born in Hobart, Tasmania, in 1938, Henry taught in secondary schools in Australia and England after receiving a Master of Arts from the University of Tasmania, and for many years was on the teaching staff in the history department of James Cook University in Townsville. He is currently Research Professor at the University of Tasmania and is the recipient of an Australian Research Council Senior Research Fellowship.

Also by Henry Reynolds

Aborigines and Settlers
Race Relations in North Queensland
The Other Side of the Frontier
Frontier
Dispossession
Black Pioneers
The Law of the Land
Aboriginal Sovereignty
This Whispering in Our Hearts
Fate of a Free People
Why Weren't We Told?
An Indelible Stain?
North of Capricorn

Nowhere People

Henry Reynolds

VIKING
an imprint of
PENGUIN BOOKS

VIKING

Published by the Penguin Group
Penguin Group (Australia)
250 Camberwell Road, Camberwell, Victoria 3124, Australia
(a division of Pearson Australia Group Pty Ltd)
Penguin Group (USA) Inc.
375 Hudson Street, New York, New York 10014, USA
Penguin Group (Canada)
90 Eglinton Avenue East, Suite 700, Toronto ON M4P 2Y3, Canada
(a division of Pearson Penguin Canada Inc.)
Penguin Books Ltd
80 Strand, London WC2R 0RL, England
Penguin Ireland
25 St Stephen's Green, Dublin 2, Ireland
(a division of Penguin Books Ltd)
Penguin Books India Pvt Ltd
11 Community Centre, Panchsheel Park, New Delhi – 110 017, India
Penguin Group (NZ)
Cnr Airborne and Rosedale Roads, Albany, Auckland, New Zealand
(a division of Pearson New Zealand Ltd)
Penguin Books (South Africa) (Pty) Ltd
24 Sturdee Avenue, Rosebank, Johannesburg 2196, South Africa

Penguin Books Ltd, Registered Offices: 80 Strand, London, WC2R 0RL, England

First published by Penguin Group (Australia), a division of Pearson Australia Group Pty Ltd, 2005

10 9 8 7 6 5 4 3 2 1

Design by Cathy Larsen © Penguin Group (Australia)
Front cover photograph: Young Aboriginal man by William Henry Corkhill, ca 1905, The William Henry Corkhill Tilba Tilba Collection, PIC TT730, by kind permission of the National Library of Australia.
Back cover photograph: Aboriginal and part-Aboriginal children in a class at the state school, La Perouse, 1959, A1200, L31898, by kind permission of the National Archives of Australia.
Back cover quote from *A Very Big Journey: my life as I remember it* by Hilda Jarman Muir, by kind permission of Aboriginal Studies Press.
Typeset in 11.5/18pt Fairfield light by Fairfield light by Midland Typesetters, Maryborough, Victoria
Printed in and bound in Australia by McPherson's Printing Group, Maryborough, Victoria

National Library of Australia
Cataloguing-in-Publication data:

Reynolds, Henry, 1938– .
Nowhere people.

Bibliography.
Includes Index.
ISBN 0 670 04118 1.

1. Reynolds, Henry, 1938– . 2. Reynolds, J, 1901– . 3. Aboriginal Australians – Mixed descent.
4. Aboriginal Australians – Mixed descent – Social conditions. 5. Racially mixed people – Australia.
6. Australia – Race relations. I. Title.

305.89915

www.penguin.com.au

For my sisters Mary and Judy
and for the grandmother we never knew

Acknowledgements

This book was written and researched while I was an
Australian Research Council Professorial Fellow at
the University of Tasmania. I am grateful to both the
Research Council and the School of History and Classics
at the university for their support and encouragement.
I have drawn heavily on the time and skill of librarians in
Australia, Britain and the United States. Over the years
I have also benefited from conversations with professional
colleagues. I should thank Peter Read for his expertise
about the stolen children; Anna Haebich for her
knowledge of fringe-dwelling communities; Marilyn Lake
for her advice about American ideas and sources; and
Russell Macgregor for his knowledge of racial
ideas in Australia. I have fruitfully discussed ideas of
miscegenation and identity with, among others, Gwen
Deemal, Jim Everett and Nicholas Shakespeare.

As this is also a book about family history, I must
record my thanks for support, encouragement
and interest received from Margaret, John, Anna and
Rebecca; from my sisters Mary and Judy and our cousin
Carolyn. I recall too with gratitude the interest shown
in our family project by my mother, the late
Isabelle Reynolds.

Terminology

Like all writers dealing with racial ideas prevalent
in the past, I have had to face the problem of
terminology. It has been necessary – and unavoidable –
to use the terms current in the periods with which
I deal, for example, 'half-caste', 'mixed blood',
'part-Aboriginal', 'mulatto', 'mestizo', etc., even
though they are now considered archaic, insulting
or offensive.

The alternative of using them constantly enclosed in
quotation marks did not seem to be an adequate
or suitable response. Even the more neutral term 'mixed
descent' carries an implication of biological determinism.
To write about race seems to necessitate using the terms
in which race was conceptualised and discussed, even
while deploring the ideas in question.

Contents

Family Secrets —

Secrets and Silences

During my many years of research into Aboriginal history, I obviously read a great deal about half-castes. I was aware of the relevant policies adopted by the various Australian governments between the 1880s and the 1960s. I had come across the innumerable derogatory comments made about people of mixed descent, having read both popular literature and the testimony of people thought to be experts at the time. But I had not set out to trace the ideas in question back to their source in the work of European and North American scholars and scientists. And I had certainly never thought that any of my research had personal relevance for me or my extended family.

But over recent years I have discovered that there was information relating to my family that I didn't know – things forgotten, details folded away in secrecy. As we began to recover these secrets, my attitude to the whole idea of the half-caste, the mestizo, began to change in sympathy. I was propelled in two quite different directions – selective excursions in intellectual history on the one hand, and family history on the other.

Where family history was concerned, there was the abiding enigma of my paternal grandmother. In that respect I had always accepted family tradition, though without much searching thought, I must admit. What we knew of her was sketchy enough. My paternal grandfather, George Rule, had left Tasmania, probably in the early 1890s, to work in an uncle's business in Sydney. He became involved and had a child with a woman who had been described at different times as an Armenian, an Indian or a Gypsy. There seemed to be consensus that she wasn't Anglo-Saxon, wasn't exactly white. My father was taken to Hobart when still a small baby, and he was raised by his Tasmanian relatives. I don't believe he ever saw his mother or father again.

My sisters and I occasionally speculated about our mysterious grandmother. Our mother Isabelle said she didn't know any more about her than we did. What we *did* know, however, was that we could never even allude to her in my father's presence. The subject was strictly taboo. When the question was inadvertently raised, his discomfort was palpable. I remember quite vividly an incident when staying with my parents in Hobart as an adult. Our elder daughter Anna, who would have been about ten at the time, had been given a sort of 'ancestor kit' including a book that allowed you to fill in relatives' names and thereby construct a family tree. My father was the obvious person to assist. He was an avid collector of material about his father's family, the Rules, and he knew a lot about them which he was always keen to share. So the task was begun with great enthusiasm. But Anna wanted to know about Dad's mother and her forebears too. And she was a persistent child. My father was acutely embarrassed, wouldn't say a word about them and the project was, for the moment, abandoned.

That incident passed and was forgotten. I gave the matter little thought until after my father's death, when my mother and elder sister Mary told me they had decided that the family secret was that our grandmother may have been part-Aboriginal. I was not quite sure what to say about this theory. I was probably dismissive, and thought the idea had emerged as a result of their reading Sally Morgan's *My Place*. I think I also felt that this was my area of expertise and I responded with a sort of miffed proprietorship. I certainly hadn't before this time given the idea a moment's consideration, although I had often been asked, by both white and Aboriginal enquirers, whether I had any Aboriginal ancestry. And I had always said no. My two sisters Mary and Judy have often been asked if they are part-Aboriginal, and I do frequently come across Aboriginal women who remind me of my sisters.

Anyhow, my mother persisted with the theory. At the time she was in a nursing home for the blind, her eyesight having seriously deteriorated. She was, however, extremely alert and was an avid listener to both the ABC and recorded books. She also spent many hours thinking about the past. So her judgement about my father's ethnicity was not to be lightly set aside. How many incidents, chance remarks, hints and allusions she had gathered up as her memory swept through the past I'm not sure. She wouldn't go into detail. You just sensed that what was at stake was much more than a passing fancy or a recently fashionable identification. She had quite clearly made up her mind.

It remained for me an interesting prospect without direct personal engagement until I was, quite by chance, looking through some old family photo albums that I hadn't opened for years. The album in question contained photos of my father when he was in his early twenties, in the early years of marriage, and took in the arrival of my elder siblings David and Mary. Many of them were small and much-faded sepia 'snaps' as they were once called. Perhaps for the first time ever, I looked at them through a magnifying glass and I was amazed at what I saw.

It wasn't just the vision of my father as a handsome young man that struck me – which indeed he was – but the fact that *he looked so Aboriginal*. Or, perhaps more precisely, manifestly part-Aboriginal. I'm aware that in itself is not really proof of anything. Facial characteristics are an uncertain guide to ancestry at the best of times. All I can say is that this pressed in upon me with great force. It was an epiphany. And the thirty years I had spent in north Queensland had sharpened my eye to the tell-tale signs of Aboriginal ancestry. It is a form of divination at which Aboriginal people themselves excel.

The second surprise that sprang from the photos was that those taken in summer indicated that unless he kept out of the sun my father went very dark. It was much more pronounced than an ordinary suntan. I immediately recalled the fact that in later life Dad was very careful to keep out of the sun, so much so that at family picnics he would walk away from the spot chosen for lunch and seek out the nearest shade – even if it was some distance away. I can remember on one occasion being very angry with him for leaving us, and I walked over to ask him why he was eating separately. He told me he just didn't like the sun.

Epiphanies notwithstanding, it wasn't much to go on. But I now had to rather sheepishly admit that my mother and sister might be onto something. Between us we began to see what we could find out. My sister talked to as many of my father's contemporaries, friends and relatives as she could find, and I engaged an experienced genealogist to see what the records might reveal. I will return to what we found in the final chapter. Meanwhile some facts about my parents will ease the reader's task.

My father was born on 16 May 1901. He was a child of a new century and a new nation. A week before he was born, the Duke of York had opened the inaugural Federal Parliament. Two days after his birth, the first wireless transmission in Australia was made. When he was quite small, Dad's mother, Margaret Dawson, took him to Hobart, left him with his father's Tasmanian relatives and then returned to Sydney to marry my grandfather. Dad was cared for by his paternal grandmother, his aunt Edith and her husband Henry Reynolds. It is not clear if it was his mother's intention to leave him with his father's Tasmanian relatives for just a short period during the early months of her marriage, or whether an intended brief island sojourn became over time a permanent one.

Nothing was officially done to regularise the arrangement between my father and his Tasmanian family. There was no formal adoption. Dad was initially known by his mother's maiden name – Dawson. Later he was called John Rule, which was his father's name, and then John Reynolds after he went to live with his aunt and her husband. Although he was known for the rest of his life as John Reynolds, he found out, when he first tried to acquire a passport, that this was not his real name. In 1959 the New South Wales Registrar General issued him with a document that regularised the situation and he officially became John Reynolds for the first time in his life.

It is known that Dad's father kept up some contact with him and apparently sent him presents on his birthdays. But I have the impression that John had been persuaded by his Tasmanian relatives that George was the black sheep of the family and had left Tasmania under a cloud. On the rare occasions Dad mentioned his father he did so with obvious embarrassment. Sadly, George committed suicide in Centennial Park in

1915, when my father was a teenager. I have no idea if Dad knew any-thing about the manner of his death or that he died almost penniless with no assets of any sort.

Although the full details of what happened during my father's early years are not recoverable, it is clear that John's Tasmanian relatives, and his step-parents Edith and Henry in particular, must have decided they would do all they could to prevent Dad from learning about his mother. To facilitate this burying of his past they had told him at some stage that he didn't have a birth certificate. I am sure that he believed this to be true. He reiterated this story in official correspondence for many years and had managed by means of it to pass over numerous bureaucratic hurdles until the problem of his needing a passport arose in 1959.

I have no doubt Dad's relatives' obfuscation and deceit were carried out with the best of intentions. They thought they were doing the right thing by him. They probably acted in this way because they knew that Margaret Dawson was what they would have called a mixed-blood or a mulatto, and the most likely scenario is that she was part-Aboriginal.

However, my impression is that the most immediate concern of Dad's paternal grandmother, uncles and aunts would have been that he had been born out of wedlock, that he was illegitimate, even though his parents subsequently married. It is hard for people today to appreciate just what a terrible stigma it was to be born a bastard. At the time many such babies were abandoned or killed to avoid the crushing weight of social opprobrium. I think the Rules may have been additionally concerned because George had already caused them social embarrassment. Hobart was a small city where in the early 1900s everyone knew everyone else's business. Gossip, social anxiety and concern about people's origins had been endemic since the era of convict transportation. The Rules did not bear the hated stain of convict ancestry, but their social standing had been achieved by education and professional advancement rather than birth, property or wealth. Their respectability, which was profoundly important to them, was fragile and insecure. As it was, Dad's aunt Edith Rule was thought to have married 'beneath her'; Henry Reynolds was a guard on the Tasmanian railways, although he later became a senior public servant with a considerable property portfolio.

Thus the sudden appearance of baby John would have taken some deft and devious explanations, if not positive deception. It is likely that his illegitimacy would have weighed more heavily with them than did his mother's uncertain origins. They were aware that she had some non-European ancestry, but they may not have been sure as to its precise nature. For her part Margaret Dawson may not even have told her husband George the truth about her heritage. She had clearly decided to 'pass' into mainstream society and leave her family ancestry behind, only too aware of what profound handicaps were imposed on Aboriginal Australians at that time.

Edith's and George's parents were well-educated, well-informed people. My great-grandfather and great-grandmother were both trained teachers and James rose during a long career to become the State Director of Education. Their daughter Edith – in effect my step-grandmother – was well-read and progressive in outlook. She would have had some understanding of contemporary thinking about race, biology and inheritance. She was a professionally trained nurse and it seems most likely that she would have been aware of all the discussion and anxiety about miscegenation. I imagine that she must have carefully watched her new charge, monitored his progress and wondered if he would manifest any undesirable characteristics; whether he would develop intellectually; and whether he would be weak and unhealthy. At the time both expert opinion and popular sentiment concurred about the degenerate nature of mixed-race people. As it turned out, Edith's presumed anxiety about John's health and intellectual development proved unfounded.

John and my mother Isabelle met in their mid-twenties in Hobart, in 1926. She had come to Tasmania to teach French and English at a private girls' school, having graduated several years before from the University of Western Australia. By then my father was a qualified industrial chemist with wide intellectual interests who had already built up an extensive library of historical and literary works. In photos taken at the time they seem to be a bright and fashionably dressed young couple who enjoyed an active social life with an equally smart group of friends. But of all the things my mother talked of in later life about that time, she returned again and again to my father's obsessive concern about his mother. She thought it was so overbearing that it was ruining his life and told him so. His anxiety must have made a vivid impression on her. It was an anecdote we children knew well, having heard it from her many times.

I wish now that I had asked her more about what my father actually said about his mother and how much he said. I wonder if Isabelle was his only confidante or whether Dad talked to his aunt and his other relatives and, if so, what they told him. Isabelle never found out how much he knew but she thought that he didn't have any concrete information about Margaret. Did he ever pursue his enquiries through the official records of the Registrar General of New South Wales? He may not have done so because there are good reasons to think that he had been convinced up until 1959 that there was no record of his birth.

I assume that like so many people separated from their parents while very young, Dad felt a strong need to at least find out about his mother. But there may have been more to it than that. His concern was probably not simply a matter of who she was, but *what* she was. In an era and in a country obsessed by race and blood, the uncertainty must have weighed heavily on him.

I don't know how concerned my father was about how he looked and if he suffered taunts about both his illegitimacy and his appearance. The latter may have mattered more to him in adulthood than the former. My impression is that he had often been hurt in this way. I am reminded of an incident when I was thirteen or fourteen that means more now than it did at the time. During one summer afternoon I looked out my half-opened bedroom window and saw my father putting a hose on the tap below the window. It was as if at that moment I suddenly saw him in an entirely different light. I said something like, 'Gee, you look just like an old darkie.' Dad looked up at me with great surprise, not knowing that I was watching him. For a brief moment I saw an expression on his face I had never seen before and would never see again. It was as if I had touched an old and very deep wound at a moment when he was for once completely off-guard and utterly vulnerable.

There was another incident that my mother often talked about in later life. It took place in Ballarat after my parents had become engaged and Mum went to teach in the central Victorian town prior to their marriage. One morning she was called unexpectedly out of class to go down to the office because a visitor had arrived to speak to her. To her complete surprise she found one of her Tasmanian friends there – a young man called Will, who I have since seen in early photos with my parents. I have an idea he may have introduced them. He explained to my mother that he had been staying in Melbourne and had come up for the day by train to speak to her. Will's mother had insisted that he see Isabelle and warn her about marrying John because his mother was a coloured woman.

It was a terribly distressing, unforgettable moment that my mother remembered vividly throughout her life. As she recounted the story to us, she angrily told Will to mind his own business and refused to discuss the matter with him. I don't think he and my father were ever reconciled. But I have no idea if Will's visit caused my mother to worry about her impending marriage or about prospective children from the union.

Looking back now, eighty years later, it is hard to understand such behaviour and the compulsion that Will and his mother felt to warn Isabelle about what must have appeared an unsuitable, even a dangerous, marriage. They no doubt felt they were looking after her best interests, protecting her from future social opprobrium. What I can't be sure about is whether this feeling was a general one in Hobart and whether Will's mother spoke for other people as well. Perhaps she was simply the one person who thought something should be done about it. But it is hard to think of anything that could have been more painful for my father, no doubt striking him at the centre of his anxieties and insecurities. Fortunately, my mother was not deterred. Had she followed the advice she was offered that morning in Ballarat my father would have felt he was cursed to become a pariah.

If Dad's Aboriginal inheritance had been commonly known and publicly acknowledged, the social pressure against the marriage would have been much more intense and might have been too great for my mother, and certainly for her parents, to bear. Social contact with a coloured woman of indeterminate origins was bad enough in the 1920s, but having a part-Aboriginal mother was another matter altogether. Isabelle's parents had both come from well-to-do middle-class families in Adelaide, later moving to Perth. Her father lost both his job and his prospects during the Depression of the 1890s and never fully recovered. The family's pressing need to assert their respectability, to stress the importance of correct speech and polite manners, was symptomatic of their long, slow decline in status which was accompanied by a dispiriting move to a smaller house in a working-class suburb, and the sale of their piano and other valuable possessions acquired in better days. They had made great sacrifices to enable Isabelle to complete secondary schooling and then go on to university. So their only child's marriage and choice of husband would have been a matter of great importance to them. However, I don't know whether Mum's parents ever expressed concern about Dad's ethnicity.

Isabelle and John were married in Perth. My father made the long journey from Tasmania by boat across Bass Strait and thence by train from Melbourne, arriving travel-worn on the morning of the wedding. I wonder now whether during the many hours spent on the train Dad worried about how he would be received by Isabelle's family and friends; whether he worried about his appearance, and if he had been keeping out of the sun so his status as a white man could not be doubted. I wonder too what Mum's friends would have made of him when he got off the train. I imagine that people in Perth were much more attuned to slight visual signs of Aboriginality than were Tasmanians. Were there whispered comments, knowing looks and raised eyebrows when Isabelle introduced her husband-to-be?

My parents grew up at a time when race was a pre-eminent concern in Western Europe and North America. It was the time when Australia was invincibly committed to a White Australia, when scarcely anyone had a good word to say for people of mixed blood – half-castes, mulattoes, mestizoes – and when the whole world seemed to be hostile to interracial marriage. The strength and provenance of these ideas must now be accounted for.

Mixed Blood

This book, then, is about people of mixed descent; those with parents or grandparents who came from different cultures; from what until recently would have been called different races. Such people were widely regarded as being part of a distinctive group known by names like mestizo, mulatto, half-breed, half-caste or mongrel. They were almost universally thought, quite literally, to have mixed blood.

Half-castes were a global phenomenon; the inevitable accompaniment of travel, trade, war and colonisation. In 1878 the distinguished anthropologist Paul Topinard estimated that 'the number of mongrels on the face of the globe' was twelve million. Eleven million were in South America alone.[1] When Brazil conducted its first national census in 1872, just over 40 per cent of the total population of ten million were people of mixed descent. In the early twentieth century there were just under 90 000 Eurasians in India. In the United States, the census takers sought to enumerate the number of mulattoes, arriving at a figure of 406 000 out of a total population of just over four million Afro-Americans in 1850. By 1910 there were two million out of just under ten million – or a little over 20 per cent of the total number of Afro-Americans.[2] At the turn of the century the activist scholar W. E. B. du Bois concluded that 'at least one third of the Negroes in the United States have distinct traces of white blood and there is also a large amount of Negro blood in the white population'.[3]

There were reports of mixed-race children among the earliest records of Portuguese and Spanish settlements in South America, West Africa, Sri Lanka and India. In both languages there were specific words for such people and often many of them, given the common complexity of ancestry and the large number of possible combinations. This was particularly true of Latin America, where intermarriage and concubinage among Europeans, Africans and Indians had been widespread from the earliest years of colonisation. An English book of 1799 provided a table of the terminology in use in the Spanish colonies:[4]

Offspring of a	Denominated	Degree of Mixture
White and Black	A Mulatto	1/2 White 1/2 Black
White and Mulatto	A Quadroon	3/4 White 1/4 Black
Black and Mulatto	A Sambo	3/4 Black 1/4 White
White and Quadroon	A Mestizo or Quinteron	7/8 White 1/8 Black
Black and Sambo	A Quinteron	7/8 Black 1/8 White
White and Mestizo	A (reputed) White	15/16 White 1/16 Black
Black and Quinteron	A (reputed) Black	15/16 Black 1/16 White

These words were always more than simple descriptive terms. They reflected a hierarchy of respect and regard, which in turn usually related to the presumed percentage of European blood. Even the Portuguese, the most racially tolerant of Europeans, discriminated against the half-caste in all their colonial outposts, referring to them as people with defective or – more specifically – infected blood, *sangre infecta*.

This should alert us to the fact that few people have suffered more opprobrium than half-castes in the European empires and their independent off-shoots. They faced deprecation and contempt from popular folk wisdom and scientific and scholarly opinion alike. There was an unusual conjunction of the demotic and the expert. Anyone who begins reading in the field will quickly become familiar with the rich vocabulary of contempt, the crowded anthology of abuse. The saying attributed to Africans by Dr Livingstone, reported by him and repeated over and over again, was that God made the white man and God made the black man, but the devil made the mulatto. An even more ubiquitous belief was that half-castes inherited the worst qualities of both parent races and the good qualities of neither. They were commonly assumed to be morally and physically defective, unpredictable, unstable and degenerate. A small selection from the vast literature of contempt will provide a quick sample from the echo chamber of abuse. Half-castes were 'poor grade humanity', 'racial mediocrities', 'poor types'. They had a 'worthless type of mind', they were 'out of adjustment to all conditions of life'. They were a 'degradation of humanity', a 'disgrace to human nature' and 'eminently bad'. One of America's leading biological scientists remarked in 1921 that the 'unfortunate cross breed' had come in for condemnation from all quarters.[5]

It is hard to adequately explain to a contemporary audience how all-pervasive these ideas were and how impossible it must have been for half-castes to counter – or even to live with – the incessant, prevailing winds of contempt. They were forever prejudged. Everyone knew what they were like. This affected not just individuals but whole communities, even countries and continents. The ubiquitous mixture of European, Indian and African in south and central America stimulated an industry of insult in North America and Western Europe that ranged in its product from disgust to amused contempt. Travellers, sociologists and scientists joined hands to write of the degenerate mixture south of the Rio Grande and to relate all of South America's troubles and turbulence to its mongrel population. An Irishman, Roger Casement, worked as a British consular official in Brazil in the early twentieth century. He was very sympathetic to the plight of the Indians, but had typical views about the mestizo population, writing:

> Heavens! What a loathsome people they are! A mixture of Jew and Nigger, and God knows what; altogether the nastiest human black pudding the world has yet cooked in her tropical stew pot.[6]

In a book entitled *Race or Mongrel* published in 1916, A. P. Schultz declared that in Peru all kinds of crossbreeds 'infested the land'. The result was 'incredible rottenness' because only the bad qualities of the whites and Negroes were 'transmitted to the mongrel offspring'.[7]

Cosmopolitan racial gossip was one thing; the invincible

certainties of experts was another. Each nourished the other. From the late eighteenth century to the mid-twentieth century, biologists, ethnographers and social commentators wrote with seeming certainty and frequent unanimity about half-castes. But for all their assumed expertise, technical skill and authoritative language, they came up with much the same sort of account that was common in popular literature. Savant and citizen were in agreement about the hapless half-castes, whose discordant bodies and minds created innumerable social problems.

But there was more to it than that. The half-caste was a threat to racial unity; they compromised the purity of blood. The further proliferation of half-castes caused anxiety in many countries in the late nineteenth and early twentieth centuries. Each census was carefully monitored to chart the growth of the evil. In the United States all mixed-blood people with any discernible trace of African or Asian ancestry were legally classified as non-white. Racial intermarriage was strictly forbidden by statute in many states and deterred by public opinion elsewhere. In Dutch and English colonies there were serious and continuous attempts to limit the breeding of half-castes by one means or another – not so much for what they did, said or thought, but for what they were.

Half-castes were, then, seen as subversive – they were biologically dangerous and therefore a threat to vital national interests. And there lay the problem. Political dissidents could change their minds, switch commitments. Religious rebels might convert or recant. But biological dissidents could do neither. Nothing could be done about one's parents and grandparents or about tainted blood. As a result governments developed an obsessive interest in half-castes, determined that it was in the national interest to stop them breeding (or to decide who they should breed with), and to take children away from parents in the name of the race and the blood of the nation. So, above all, it was the young women who mattered and who were seen as the inadvertent biological revolutionaries who had to be watched, managed and controlled.

Concern with race and blood linked many parts of the world at the turn of the nineteenth century – Western Europe, Britain, the United States, Canada, Australia, New Zealand, South Africa – and white colonial minorities in the many outposts of European empires. The ideas and theories about race were principally crafted in Europe and the United States, the phrases coined, the books and articles written. The accounts of explorers, travellers and settlers and the bones and skulls of indigenous people flowed back from the frontiers of Empire to the museums, universities and studies of the great metropolitan centres.

Interracial sex and the creation of mixed-race children were the focal points on which all the anxieties about the future health of the race concentrated. In the early twentieth century both expert and popular opinions vehemently opposed miscegenation (although there were always a few dissidents who spoke in favour of racial mingling and were regarded as eccentrics for their trouble). A British medical specialist declared in 1906 that intermarriage between his countrymen and non-Europeans should be prevented because along with his colleagues he knew of the 'terrible monstrosities' produced by such unions.[8]

The South African statesman J. C. Smuts informed an influential audience in London in 1917 that it was a fundamental axiom that in Africa there must be 'no intermixture of blood between the two colours'. Few of his listeners would have disagreed with him.[9] Even contemporaries of Smuts who urged an easing of South Africa's evolving policies of segregation were anxious not to be seen as proponents of miscegenation, so unacceptable was it and so subversive would it be to one's detailed and substantial arguments. The retired colonial administrator and explorer Harry Johnston urged a change of direction for South Africa in an article in 1924, which, however, concluded with the following passage: 'Then comes the crucial question – "So you approve of miscegenation, of the production of mulatto people, mixed races between Black and White?"' Johnston's reply was telling:

> Well no. I cannot say I *approve* of our losing our pink and white complexions and our position as highest race. I do not welcome the idea of extreme types mingling and producing a hybrid.[10]

In popular discussions right up until recent times there was one revealing, ubiquitous retort to any talk of racial equality: 'That's all very well in theory, but you wouldn't want your daughter to marry one.'

Australia produced its own contemptuous discourse. It was distinctive but certainly not unique. Half-caste was the term most widely used, regardless of the specific details of a targeted person's descent. But it was quite common to call mixed-descent people mongrels, a term which was also used to describe morally worthless, contemptible individuals. The Administrator of the Northern Territory declared in an official report in 1915 that it was 'freely stated' that all half-castes were morally worthless, that the 'taint was in them, and that it must inevitably manifest itself'.[11] In 1928 the *Brisbane Mail* called half-castes a 'pathetic, sinister third race'.[12] Gilbert White, the distinguished Anglican Bishop of Carpentaria, believed that if they were not taken in hand they were likely to become 'one of the most dangerous elements in the whole community'.[13] But there were few as hostile to half-castes as Daisy Bates, for many people in the first half of the twentieth century the leading authority on the Aborigines. Isobel White, who edited Bates's *The Native Tribes of Western Australia*, observed that she abominated the very idea of sexual relations between Europeans and Aborigines and that the resultant progeny were despised by her.[14] 'As to the half-caste,' Bates wrote in a Western Australian paper in 1921, 'however early they may be taken and trained, with very few exceptions, the only good half-caste is a dead one.'[15]

Australian policies showed the often unattributed influence of major intellectual figures of the Atlantic world. It is not surprising, then, that the half-caste was central to government thinking in the antipodes between the 1880s and the 1940s. White Australia differentiated sharply between the half-caste and the full blood. It was universally understood that the full blood was dying out. Metropolitan theory proclaimed what local knowledge could confirm. Meagre welfare measures were appropriate in order to ameliorate the last days of a dying people. Eventually reserves were created to allow traditional people to live out their shrinking time without undue interference or unnecessary expense.

But the half-caste was a different matter altogether. By the early twentieth century it was apparent that they were not dying out, regardless of what was happening with their full-blood relatives. In fact numbers were increasing, the population was youthful and families were large, despite poverty and deprivation. This was unexpected. Alarmed observers often couldn't hide their surprise. They might have been less startled if they had bothered to consider the demographic evidence in other parts of the world where indigenous populations had recovered after long periods of decline. And it need not have caused concern. In different circumstances it might have been the occasion for celebration – even of jubilation. But Australia at the time of Federation was obsessed with blood and biology and was committed head and heart to a White Australia. It could not find any pleasure in a swelling half-caste population.

And it saw the phenomenon as mainly a biological one. Officials began to count indigenous Australians and to divide them into full blood and half-caste, and often differentiated again between half-caste, quadroon and octoroon. Running parallel with enumeration came the observation of fair-haired, European-looking children living in the Aboriginal camps. Politicians and officials began to implement policies that cut through the web of kinship that linked indigenous people, regardless of colour or blood. They removed increasing numbers of men, women and children to closed and normally isolated reserves. They took children away from their parents, uncles and aunts, to be raised in dormitories or in institutions far from their homes. So much was sacrificed on the altar of White Australia and for the nation's grand passion for racial purity.

Nothing so clearly illustrated the powerlessness of Aboriginal people than the manner in which they were defined and categorised by settler society, its officials and governments. The people who saw themselves as members of hundreds of distinctive language groups or nations all became 'Aborigines', to be regarded and treated alike. Post-settlement communities found themselves divided into full bloods and half-castes, although such categorisations rarely meant as much to them as their powerful webs of kinship with their elaborate codes of conduct and etiquette that encompassed individuals regardless of whether they had a non-indigenous father or grandfather.

In recent times Australian governments have adopted a definition of Aboriginality taken from United Nations reports that attempted to provide a means of determining indigenousness all over the world. There were three requirements – biological descent from indigenous forebears; identification with an indigenous community; and acceptance by such a group. The definition was adopted at a time when there was growing federal government engagement in Aboriginal affairs and when it became necessary to determine who could vote for and hold office in indigenous organisations and have access to a range of specific programs, services and grants.

Like all previous definitions, it has created many problems relating to identity which became less a matter of private engagement than a form of public labelling. Many individuals had great difficulty when forced by the logic of government policy to decide whether they were indigenous or non-indigenous, black or white, although colour itself is often no help in facilitating definitions. In recent years the Aboriginality of prominent figures in the indigenous movement has been questioned. In Tasmania, for example, there is deep and bitter conflict about who is and who isn't

Aboriginal. A federal court case in 1998 failed to find a way to provide a satisfactory definition of Aboriginality. The descendants of indentured Melanesian labourers have faced similar problems. They have a strong sense of community, of being Pacific Islanders, but some families have Aboriginal grandmothers or great-grandmothers. Some people claiming Aboriginal descent have achieved prominent positions in indigenous organisations, while others have been rebuffed and have been denied access to programs and grants.

The coloured communities of north Australia which have Afghan, Chinese, Japanese or Malaysian ancestry at various times often incorporated Aboriginal women in temporary liaisons or long-term relationships. Their descendants' problem is whether they should claim to be Aboriginal and privilege just one branch of their often complicated family tree. Such people of mixed – or complicated – descent have at times been attacked from two directions. If they don't identify as Aboriginals they are accused of denying or disowning their heritage. When they do they are often challenged as to the legitimacy of their access to services and grants.

These are just some of the contemporary problems that can be traced back to the racial thought and resulting definitions which, as we will see, were characteristic of both Australia and much of the Western world in the late nineteenth and early twentieth centuries.

PART 1 | Ideas from Overseas

CHAPTER 1

The Ball and Chain of Hybridism

People of mixed descent were discussed in many books written in Europe and North America in the eighteenth and nineteenth centuries. Travellers returning home from overseas colonies told tales about the mulattoes and mestizoes they had encountered on their travels. They were featured in the same way as picturesque landscapes and exotic animals and plants. They rarely received good press and were commonly treated with contempt – sometimes as figures of fun, but more often as grotesque human anomalies. A typical and influential book was Edward Long's three-volume *History of Jamaica*, published in London in 1774. The author called on his readers to turn their eyes to the Spanish American dominions, 'and behold what a vicious, brutal, and degenerate breed of mongrels has been there produced, between Spaniards, Blacks, Indians and their mixed progeny'.[1]

The concern about racial mixture was also apparent in Thomas Jefferson's *Notes on the State of Virginia* of 1788. He believed that the blacks were inferior to Europeans in 'the endowments both of body and mind'. Their 'unfortunate difference of colour and faculty' was a powerful obstacle to emancipation which would, if uncontrolled, lead to racial mixture. In the prior case of Roman slave emancipation, it required 'but one effort'. The emancipated slave could mix with the free citizens 'without staining the blood of his master'. But in Virginia a second step would be necessary, unknown to history. When the African was freed, it was essential that he be 'removed beyond the reach of mixture'.[2]

When Jefferson was writing, Virginia had laws prohibiting racial intermarriage that had been in operation for a hundred years. A statute of 1691 was drafted to prevent 'that abominable mixture and spurious issue' that resulted from Negroes, mulattoes and Indians intermarrying with 'English or other white women'. A later Act for 'The Better Preventing of a Spurious and Mixt Issue' declared

> if any Negro or molatto [sic] man shall commit fornication with an English woman, or a woman of any other Christian nation within this province both offenders shall be severely whip'd [and the] man shall be ordered to be sold out of the province . . . within the space of six months.[3]

During the first half of the nineteenth century the question of racial mixture became entangled within a much larger debate about the diversity and origin of humanity, one often characterised as conflict between monogenesists and polygenesists. The central issue at stake was whether humankind was one species or several. It was a debate that inevitably took on theological colouring, the monogenesists referring to the biblical account of Genesis and drawing the conclusion that all people were descended from Adam and Eve, were of one blood and made in the image of God. Demonstrable racial differences were the product of social circumstances and geographical diversity, but no matter how great the gulf separating peoples they were all one species and therefore able to breed successfully together. In his *On the Natural Variety of Mankind*, first published in 1776, J. F. Blumenbach observed that 'no doubt can any longer remain but that we are with great probability right in referring all and singular as many varieties of man as are at present known to one and the same species'.[4]

The monogenesist position claimed the allegiance of the majority of scholars in Britain during the first half of the nineteenth century and was strongly championed by the leading ethnographer, J. C. Prichard. Prichard observed that if the 'Negro and the Australian' were not our fellow creatures and of one family with ourselves but 'beings of an inferior order', then the relations with Europeans would not be very different from those that might be imagined to exist 'between us and a race of orang-utans'.[5] 'The Sacred Scriptures', he wrote,

> declare that it pleased the Almighty Creator to make of one blood all the nations of the earth, and that all mankind are the offspring of common parents. But there are writers in the present day who maintain that this assertion does not comprehend the uncivilised inhabitants of remote regions; and that Negroes, Hottentots, Esquimaux, and Australians, are not, in fact, men in the full sense of the term, or beings endowed with like mental faculties as ourselves. Some of these writers contend that the races above mentioned, and other rude and barbarous tribes, are inferior in

ndowments to the human family which supplied
ope and Asia with inhabitants – that they are organically
different and can never be raised to an equality, in moral and
intellectual powers, with the offspring of that race which displays
in the highest degree all the attributes of humanity. They maintain that the ultimate lot of the ruder tribes is a state of perpetual
servitude, and that, if in some [places] they should continue to
repel the attempts of the civilized nations to subdue them, they
will at length be rooted out and exterminated in every country on
the shores of which Europeans should set their feet. These half
man half brutes were made to be domestic slaves of the lordly
caste, under whose protection they are susceptible of some small
improvement, comparable to what is attained by our horses
and dogs.[6]

The great importance of these seemingly arcane debates for
the future of slavery and the course of European colonisation will
be immediately apparent. So too was the discussion about miscegenation. If all humankind was one species then all people could
intermarry and produce fertile and healthy offspring. If, on the
other hand, the polygenesists were right, then intermarriage was
unnatural; sexual intercourse across the colour line was akin to
bestiality and if any children were produced they could be
expected to be unhealthy, degenerate and infertile. The debate
had an enormous bearing on judgements made about mixed-blood
people all over the world and about whole countries where interracial mixing was commonplace. Prichard's view on the matter
was clear. He wrote:

[I]t may be asserted without the least chance of contradiction, that mankind, of all races and varieties are equally capable of propagating their offspring by intermarriages and that such connexions are equally prolific whether contracted between individuals of the same or of the most dissimilar varieties. If there is any difference, it is probably in favour of the latter.[7]

But while British anatomists and ethnographers of Prichard's generation remained committed to monogenesis and, as a corollary, believed that different races could interbreed, they did not necessarily consider that the outcome was favourable for Europeans. In his widely read *Lectures on Comparative Anatomy* (which went through nine editions between 1819 and 1844), William Lawrence observed that in colour, figure and moral qualities the mulatto was 'a medium between the European and the African' and in 'cleanliness, activity and courage . . . decidedly superior to the Negroes'. But the mulatto was inferior to the European, Lawrence observed:

Where several races are brought together, as in some parts of the Spanish America, and in some European-Asiatic settlements, their mixtures with each other, and the several crossings between the original races and their various descendants, give rise to a vast number of mixed breeds, and every possible variety of colour. The dark races, and all who are contaminated by any visible mixture of dark blood, are comprised under the general denomination of people of colour. It is not, however, merely by this superficial character that they are distinguished; all other physical and moral qualities are equally influenced by those of the parents. The intellectual and moral character of the Europeans is deteriorated by the mixture of black or red blood, while on the other hand the infusion of white blood tends, in an equal degree, to improve and ennoble the qualities of the dark variety.[8]

Polygenisists rarely had a good word to say for racial mixture. While their opponents thought that non-Europeans could be improved by miscegenation, they were pessimistic about any successful racial mixture at all. They believed that racial differences were so striking that they must have been foundational, that the observed physical differences were so great that they could not have developed within the assumed lapse of time between the creation and the present of only 6000 years. The conclusion must be that the different races had been created separately and could not, therefore, be regarded as belonging to one species.

Much of the intellectual drive behind these ideas came from the West Indies and the southern states of the American union. Their value for providing justification for slavery was apparent at the time and widely acknowledged. Both Edward Long and Thomas Jefferson believed that Africans had been created as a separate race, Long arguing that there were 'very potent reasons for believing that the White and Negroes are two distinct species'. This being so, Long endeavoured to prove that any union between the two was likely to be barren. If children did appear, they would prove both degenerate and infertile.[9]

By the middle of the nineteenth century the monogenesists and advocates of underlying racial equality were in retreat. In her authoritative study *The Idea of Race in Science: Great Britain, 1800–1960*, Nancy Stepan observed:

> A fundamental question about the history of racism in the first half of the nineteenth century is why it was that, just as the battle against slavery was being won by abolitionists, the war against racism in European thought was being lost . . . Nowhere was racialism more apparent than in science. By 1850, racial science was far less universalistic, egalitarian and humanistic in outlook than it had been in 1800. A fundamental re-orientation had in fact taken place.[10]

During the 1850s a number of influential books were published in Europe and America that emphasised racial inequality, the similarity between Africans, Aborigines and monkeys, and the dangers of miscegenation. In 1854 Arthur de Gobineau's *The Inequality of Human Races* preached a powerful lesson against racial degeneration and the 'continual adulteration' produced by inappropriate intermarriage.[11] In the same year the American ethnographers J. C. Nott and G. R. Gliddon published their large work *Types of Mankind*, and argued similarly that the superior races should be kept 'free from adulteration'; otherwise they would degrade instead of advancing in civilisation.[12] In a later paper Nott was more emphatic, declaring that it was certain that the white race was 'deteriorated by every drop of black blood infiltrated into it' just as surely as the blood of the greyhound or pointer was polluted by the cur.[13]

In 1856 the controversial Scottish surgeon Robert Knox published his polemical work *The Races of Man: A Philosophical Enquiry Into the Influence of Race Over the Destiny of Nations.*

He had no doubt about the nature of the hybrid, which was 'a degradation of humanity and was rejected by nature'. Like many of his contemporaries, Knox was horrified by the racial mixture in Latin America, whose Hispano-hybrid races were 'a disgrace to human nature'. He believed that the hybrid produced between the male European and the female Australian was altogether sterile from the first.[14]

The prominent American zoologist Louis Aggasiz responded in a similar way to the 'evil of the mixture of races'. When visiting Brazil with its large mixed-race population he concluded that while each race in question – European, African and Indian – had distinctive qualities and characteristics, they were confused and lost in mulatto offspring. Brazil was seen as a sort of social laboratory where race mixing had been going on without restraint over many generations. The first national census of 1872 indicated that 42 per cent of just under ten million people were of mixed ancestry. Aggasiz reacted with horror and disdain, writing in his bestselling book of 1868, A Journey in Brazil, that the

> natural result of an uninterrupted contact of half-breeds with one another is a class of men in which pure type fades away as completely as do all the good qualities, physical and moral, of the primitive races, engendering a mongrel crowd as repulsive as the mongrel dogs, which are apt to be their companions.[15]

Such reactions were not uncommon among scientists and ethnographers in the middle of the nineteenth century. In his On the Phenomena of Hybridity, Paul Broca considered the characteristics of mulattoes in the West Indies, South America, Mexico,

Mauritius and Senegal, and concluded that they were very often inferior to the two parent stocks in vitality, intelligence and morality. The 'negro-indian mix' of Peru and Nicaragua formed the worst class of citizen in those countries, while in Australia racial mixture had produced 'inferior cross breeds'.[16] Another French scholar, Georges Pouchet, came to very similar conclusions. He believed that a hybrid race could only have an ephemeral existence and its intellectual condition was not much more satisfactory. When two very different races were united 'we must not hope for anything good or durable from their union'.[17]

In an American survey entitled *Indigenous Races of the Earth*, J. A. Meigs provided a detailed assessment of the results of amalgamation between races 'remote' from one another. The hybrids in question were weak, short-lived and prone to disease. With mulattoes the lateral expansion of the head ceased in infancy, he wrote, making them narrow-headed and degenerate. Even when the mulattoes were absorbed back into the white population they left behind a legacy 'in the shape of malformation – modifications of the skull, stature and intelligence'. Mulattoes illustrated a 'confusion of forms'. Nature did not tolerate racial mixing. She asserted her dominion, and manifested her disapproval in deterioration and degradation, the depopulating consequences of which were 'appalling to contemplate'.[18]

Racial thought was deeply influenced – and often in complex and conflicting ways – by the evolutionary ideas of Charles Darwin as expressed most significantly in his *Origin of the Species* of 1859 and *The Descent of Man* of 1872. The long-running controversy of monogenesists and polygenesists was then superseded by the new synthesis that assumed that the different races had evolved into their present form over very long periods of time. The Darwinians did not doubt the centrality of race. Darwin's cousin Francis Galton believed that the 'very foundation and outcome of the human mind is dependent on race'.[19] The idea of a racial hierarchy was also taken over from earlier ethnographers and given new lustre. The distinctive qualities of the different races were the product of their history. It was no longer a matter of being higher or lower on a chain of being but being more or less recently evolved, being archaic or modern, being in an evolutionary sense closer or more remote from man's primate cousins.

It might have been thought that people of mixed blood would have fared better in the hands of the Darwinians. But such was not the case. The new thinking was just as corrupted by old and deep prejudices as what had been replaced. Darwinian biology and sociology expressed the same concern about miscegenation and drew as readily on the tales told by travellers returning from exotic locations. The new science was mixed with scuttlebutt and scandal. Nancy Stepan observed that the theory that improper racial mixing resulted in degeneracy 'had a very long life, surviving countless changes in biological theory'.[20]

Herbert Spencer was probably the most widely read and influential thinker who applied evolutionary ideas to society. But he adopted many of the prejudices of the polygenesists, believing that while mating among Europeans produced good results, the union of divergent people produced 'a worthless type of mind' fitted neither to the life led by the higher or the lower race, a mind 'out of adjustment to all conditions of life'.[21] Darwin was no kinder to the mulatto, believing that 'crossed races of men are singularly savage and degraded' and that when two races 'both low on the scale' were crossed, the progeny seemed 'eminently bad'.[22] He drew on statements 'so frequently made by travellers in all parts of the world' on the degraded state and savage disposition of 'crossed races of men'. He recalled in later life his earlier travels in South America when he was struck by the impression that men of 'complicated descent' seldom had a good expression on their face. Having quoted the opinion of other eminent – and prejudiced – travellers, Darwin concluded from what he called 'these facts' that it was appropriate to infer 'that the degraded state of so many half-castes is in part due to reversion to a primitive and savage condition, induced by the act of crossing, as well as to the unfavourable moral conditions under which they generally exist'.[23]

American experience of slavery, the Civil War and Reconstruction thrust questions about race and miscegenation to the forefront of both scientific and sociological enquiry, even while local theorists drew on ideas first minted in Europe. The mobilisation of tens of thousands of young men for war enabled scientists to carry out large-scale assessment of both individuals and racial types. Using a range of the latest anatomical devices, the United States Sanitary Commission examined almost 16 000 men, measuring head and body size, strength, vision, hearing, respiration and lung capacity. The survey included over 2000 Afro-Americans and 863 mulattoes. In their official report the Commissioners confirmed the claims of earlier theorists – mulattoes were physically inferior to the 'pure' races and lacked vitality, strongly confirming pre-existing prejudices against miscegenation.[24]

Leading American scientists working between the Civil War and the end of the century arrived at the same destination by a variety of intellectual paths. Joseph le Conte, a prominent polymath, was a strong opponent of racial mixture, believing that it was not merely undesirable but against the grain of nature, a fact confirmed by the limited fertility of resulting offspring. In an article of 1893 entitled 'Race Problem in the South', he outlined the situation:

> In some there is offspring, but the offspring is a sterile hybrid which dies without issue. In some the hybrid is fertile, but its offspring is feeble, and therefore quickly eliminated in the struggle for life with the pure stock, and becomes extinct in a few generations.[25]

Nathaniel Southgate Shaler was another eminent scientist who, among other things, became concerned with racial science, miscegenation and alien immigration. He too was convinced that the only solution was to preserve the purity of both white and black races and to keep them segregated. The mulatto was, therefore, both a biological and a political threat. He was like 'the man of most mixed races', particularly inflammable, combining both a sense of grievance and a laxity of morals. But the long-term prospect was good because Shaler believed that miscegenation was declining in the late nineteenth century, and the mulatto was short-lived and unfruitful.[26]

In 1896 the statistician F. L. Hoffman published his *Race Traits and Tendencies of the American Negro*, which brought together much of the medical and ethnographic research of the previous half-century – and many of the prejudices and preoccupations of

American intellectuals of the period. Like many of his colleagues, Hoffman approved of intermarriage between closely related peoples but was a determined opponent of intermarriage or concubinage between white and black, believing that the offspring of such unions was inferior to the parents both physically and morally. While studies suggested that the mulatto had superior intellectual attainments to the Afro-American, this in no way compensated for the 'overburdening deterioration in physical and moral capacity'. Hoffman was convinced that miscegenation was detrimental to both white and black. The conclusion, therefore, was unavoidable that

> the amalgamation of the two races through the channels of prostitution or concubinage, as well as through the intermarrying of the lower types of both races, is contrary to the interest of the colored race, a positive hindrance to its social, mental and moral development. But aside from these considerations, important as they are, the physiological consequences alone demand race purity and a stern reprobation of any infusion of white blood.[27]

The mulatto, then, was a grave threat to Afro-Americans. For their sake miscegenation must be curtailed.

American social scientists were equally hostile to miscegenation. The distinguished ethnographer D. G. Brinton believed it was a question that touched the whole world 'and very closely'. Indeed, he knew of nothing 'more decisive for the future prosperity or failure of the human species' than the effect of 'race-intermarriage'. Mulattoes, he believed, were deficient in physical vigour, prone to scrofula and consumption and were unable to bear hard work. The third generation of descendants of a marriage between a white and a Polynesian, an Australian or a Dravidian 'became extinct through short lives, feeble constitutions or sterility'. A white man who took in marriage a woman of a darker race entailed 'indelible degradation on his descendants'.[28] The pioneer sociologist E. O. Ross declared that the superiority of the white race could not be preserved without pride of blood and an 'uncompromising attitude towards the lower races'. In Latin America the Portuguese and Spaniards had shown far less of 'that race aversion' that was so characteristic of the Dutch and the English. Consequently, the whole of central and south America would for centuries 'drag the ball and chain of hybridism'.[29]

CHAPTER 2 | # Fear of

Miscegenation

Attitudes to people of mixed descent did not improve much during the first third of the twentieth century, although there were always thinkers who dissented from racist orthodoxies. New theories and techniques – eugenics, genetics, statistics and intelligence tests – were used to buttress entrenched prejudices.

The old timeworn sayings and the enduring nuggets of folk wisdom were still in circulation, and still taken for granted – half-castes inherited the worst qualities of both races; they were unstable and degenerate; they were rejected by all. Truisms repeated so often were assumed to be true. Proof was not required. Unaccompanied assertion was sufficient. So a bill presented to the New Jersey State legislature in 1927 could declare in its preamble that

> [t]he intermarriage of white people and Negroes produces a mongrel breed often acquiring the vices of both races and virtues of neither . . . [they] are held in contempt by members of both the white and Negro races . . .[1]

The Michigan Board of Health published a pamphlet in 1913 written by Dr V. C. Vaughan, the dean of the State's medical school, which announced that interracial marriage produced undesirable progeny. The Eurasians of India, the mulattoes of the United States and the mixed races of South America were, he declared, 'unanswerable arguments against race mixtures'. The bad of each side became dominant 'and the mongrel, whether man or beast, is no credit to the pure blood on either side of the house'.[2]

Such resilient, deep-rooted intellectual undergrowth would have been difficult enough to deal with, but there was also a crowd of experts whose evidence had to be considered – buttressing old notions with the gleaming products of new science. Much of what had been written before 1900 continued to have currency. Scholars went on measuring heads and skulls and brains with even greater attention and sophistication in their search for precise definitions of racial difference. The idea that the races were separate species continued to find distinguished advocates. Despite all the evidence to the contrary, books were published arguing that mixed-blood people were destined to die out. A scholar writing in the *American Journal of Sociology* in 1905 argued that the preceding few years had witnessed a great change of mind 'in matters of humanitarianism'. The absolute unity of human life in all parts of the globe 'as well as the idea of the practical equality of human individuals . . . has been quite generally abandoned'.[3]

The continuity of ideas from the late nineteenth century into the early twentieth century can be illustrated by a remarkable letter written in 1892 by the eminent and elderly British philosopher

Herbert Spencer to Count Ito, who had recently been appointed prime minister of Japan. It was a private letter and Spencer insisted that it not be published during his lifetime (presumably the Japanese were not fully aware of European and American attitudes). Ito had asked the Englishman for advice about the possible intermarriage of Japanese and foreigners. Spencer was emphatic:

> It should be positively forbidden. It is not at root a question of social philosophy. It is at root a question of biology. There is abundant proof, alike furnished by the intermarriages of human races and by the interbreeding of animals, that when the varieties mingled diverge beyond a certain slight degree *the result is invariably a bad one* in the long run. I have myself been in the habit of looking at the evidence bearing on this matter for many years past, and my conviction is based upon numerous facts derived from numerous sources. This conviction I have within the last half-hour verified, for I happen to be staying in the country with a gentleman who is well-known as an authority on horses, cattle and sheep, and knows much respecting their interbreeding; and he has just, on inquiry, fully confirmed my belief that when, say of different varieties of sheep, there is an interbreeding *of those which are widely unlike*, the result, especially in the second generation, is a bad one – there arises an incalculable mixture of traits and what may be called a chaotic constitution. And the same thing happens among human beings – Eurasians in India and the half-breeds in America, show this. The physiological basis of this experience appears to be that any one variety of creature in course of many generations acquires a certain constitutional

adaptation to its particular form of life, and every other variety similarly acquires its own special adaptation. The consequence is that, if you mix the constitutions of two widely divergent varieties which have severally become adapted to widely divergent modes of life, you get a constitution which is adapted to the mode of life of neither – a constitution which will not work properly, because it is not fitted for any set of conditions whatever. By all means, therefore, peremptorily interdict marriages of Japanese with foreigners.

I have for the reasons indicated entirely approved of the regulations which have been established in America for restraining the Chinese immigration and had I the power would restrict them to the smallest possible amount, my reasons for this decision being that one of two things must happen. If the Chinese are allowed to settle extensively in America, they must either, if they remain unmixed form a subject race in the position, if not of slaves, yet of a class approaching to slaves; or if they mix they must form a bad hybrid. In either case, supposing the immigration to be large, immense social mischief must arise and eventually social disorganization. The same thing will happen if there should be any considerable mixture of the European or American races with the Japanese. You see, therefore, that my advice is strongly conservative in all directions, and I end by saying as I began – *keep other races at arm's length as much as possible.*

The letter was reproduced by the distinguished British geographer J. W. Gregory in his 1925 book *The Menace of Colour.*[4] He argued that Spencer was advancing a proposition widely accepted by contemporary experts in Britain and abroad. It had simply been ahead of its time in 1892.

The old certainties were now given new, contemporary explanations. Of direct relevance to the matter of race was the work that brought together the new discipline of statistics with studies of genetic inheritance, both at the forefront of intellectual endeavour in the early years of the twentieth century. One of the most prominent workers in the field was Charles Davenport, who became the director of what was called the Eugenics Record Office established at Cold Spring Harbour in New York in 1910. In a 1917 paper on 'The Effects of Race Intermingling', Davenport began with the assumption that long-established races were well adapted to their environments and their 'parts and functions' were harmoniously adjusted. But miscegenation produced disharmony of physical, mental and temperamental qualities. Hybrids were simply unfortunate mixtures. They were 'a badly put together people' who suffered from 'bodily maladjustment'. They were also people with turbulent characters, being dissatisfied, restless and ineffective. Davenport believed that such internal mental and temperamental friction led to crime and insanity. He illustrated what he believed were the principles involved by reporting his experiments with breeding poultry, mating a Leghorn, which laid eggs continuously, with a Brahina, which was not as effective as an egg producer but was an excellent mother. The hybrid offspring was a failure both as an egg layer and as a brooder of chickens.[5]

Davenport's most ambitious work was on racial mixture in Jamaica, where he carried out as many as seventy-eight distinctive tests on fifty men and fifty women from each of what he considered the three main groups – black, white and brown. The research came in with utterly predictable answers. The whites were superior on most indicators. The mulattoes were more intelligent than the black subjects but they were uniquely handicapped by physical and mental disharmonies. A greater number of them than among either blacks or whites were what Davenport termed 'muddled or wuzzle headed'. And while they showed precocious development as children, the great social difficulty was that they failed to progress beyond the adolescent stage.[6]

Similar work by kindred scholars in different parts of the world came up with comparable results. Vaughan MacCaughey published his study *Race Mixture in Hawaii* in 1919. He believed that the children of Caucasians and Hawaiians seemed to 'blend the least desirable traits of both parents'. In fact most marriages between Europeans and North Americans with dark-skinned peoples were 'biologically wasteful'. The large half-white population that had sprung up wherever the white man had gone among dark-skinned peoples testified 'to the enormous squandering of the hereditary physical, psychic and racial traits of the North European'.[7]

A. M. Eastabrook and I. E. McDougle studied an isolated community of 'Indian-negro-white crosses' who had lived in the same locality for over a hundred years. They called their book *Mongrel Virginians*. The so-called mongrels were below average mentally and socially. They were lacking in academic ability, were lazy and incapable of benefiting from training. All in all, the general level of the white was 'lowered in this mixture'.[8]

In Norway J.A. Mjoen of the Winderen Laboratory in Oslo

carried out a series of tests on selected groups of Scandinavians, Sami and mulattoes in the sub-arctic north. He compared 600 Swedes, 600 Sami and 300 hybrids. He didn't have a good word for the hybrids. They were inferior physically and mentally. 'Whole families of this hybrid population', he declared, were filling up the prisons and asylums. Their putative degeneracy was due to their being a 'badly mixed race', having all the characteristics of 'unbalanced hybrids'. But there were even greater matters to consider. Any crossings between widely different races could lower their physical and mental level. Unrestricted racial mixture was 'building a wide conduit . . . for a blood mixture between the two races' that society would 'eventually deplore and regret'.[9]

The belief that mixed-race people were disharmonious runs through much of the relevant scientific literature of the early twentieth century. Experiments with animals and plants were frequently referred to. Mjoen bred rabbits from widely different stock and triumphantly displayed to his colleagues a hapless animal with one ear cocked and the other one flopped down on its furry head. This appeared to be highly relevant, because it was assumed that hybrids combined ill-assorted physical characteristics. There are references in the literature to subjects having teeth too big for their jaws, or jaws too big for the teeth, of hearts and lungs too small for the frame, of short arms not matching long legs. Indeed, in a 'cross of different races' the human biologist of the period expected to see 'jumbles of anatomical characteristics'.[10] The Harvard scholar Edward East, perhaps the most highly regarded expert on racial mixture, observed that it was a 'bold tinker' who wished to try his hand at exchanging parts. The stockbreeder, East observed, needed no argument to oppose the practice. While he realised the possibilities in hybridisation, he laughed down the man who suggested hybridising 'the Jersey and the Hereford'.[11]

The assumed physical disharmony could be explored by using a battery of tests measuring arms and legs, hands and feet, fingers and toes, skulls, faces and noses among large numbers of patient subjects who were no doubt assured they were helping the cause of innovative science. William McDougall, the prominent pioneer of social psychology, was convinced that an inharmonious combination of physical features was 'characteristic of the mongrel'. But his field of study was the mind, not the body. He wrote the standard textbook *Social Psychology*, which was reprinted many times during the early decades of the twentieth century. While conceding that it was impossible to directly observe and measure the disharmonies of mental constitution, he believed there were good reasons to believe they existed. As everyone knew, the soul of the crossbreed was apt to be the scene of perpetual conflict of inharmonious tendencies. McDougall conceded there wasn't any hard evidence to support this contention, but it had been the theme of many stories and there was no reason to doubt that they were founded on close observation and in the main depicted actual experience. However, it was on the moral, rather than the intellectual, side of the mind that disharmony made itself felt most strongly. The crossbreed was detached from the moral traditions of both parent stocks and could assimilate neither tradition as easily or completely as the purebred person.[12]

McDougall arrived at the same position as many of his contemporaries in a variety of disciplines. The crossing of 'closely allied stocks' generally produced a 'blended sub-race superior to the mean of the two parental stocks, or at least not inferior'. But no such happy result was produced by the crossing of the most widely different stocks. That process produced an inferior race. McDougall admitted that unfortunately this generalisation could not at the time be based on exact and firmly established data, but it was in harmony with 'old established popular beliefs' and with what was known of the crossing of animal breeds. It was borne out by 'a general inspection of many examples'. The centuries-old blending of stocks in South America had resulted in a sub-race 'inferior to the parent races'. The mulattoes of North America and the West Indies were superior in some senses to the pure Negroes but they were deficient in vitality and fertility and the race could not maintain itself. For their part the Eurasians of India were commonly said to be 'a comparatively feeble people', while the blend of Caucasian with the yellow race was generally a poor type. McDougall reported that examples abounded in Java of people of mixed Javanese and Dutch blood and they were for the most part 'feeble specimens of humanity'.[13]

Miscegenation not only produced feeble specimens, it also undermined the stability of established races which, through centuries of adaptation, had built up efficient physical and psychic mechanisms. The machinery of the various races had been 'smoothed into an easy-running whole' by the very fact of survival during the last half a million years. There were a series of character complexes built up through ages of selection which were compatible with one another.[14] Edward East and Donald Jones explained that the result of wide racial crosses was to 'break apart' those compatible physical and mental qualities that had established 'a smoothly operating whole in each race by generations of natural selection'. Through the operation of the laws of heredity such cross-race unions tended

> to break apart series of character complexes which through years of selection have proved to be compatible with each other and with the persistence of the race under the environment to which it has been subjected.

In the genetic mixture accompanying miscegenation there was a low probability of obtaining a 'single recombination equal or superior to the average of the better race'. Interracial mixing could not possibly warrant the inevitable production of 'multitudes of racial mediocrates'.[15]

Although they wrote and spoke of the integrity of the world's main racial groups, the deepest concern of British and American biologists, psychologists and ethnographers was with maintaining what they termed the 'purity' of the white race. 'The inheritance of a superior race', S. J. Holmes, the professor of zoology at the University of California, wrote in 1923, 'is a very precious possession to be conserved at all costs'. Caution was essential because if as a result of widespread intermarriage a considerable proportion of the 'first racial cross' should prove to be 'undesirable products', as one might reasonably expect, the damage would take a long time to remedy. The bad blood would be difficult to expel, Holmes argued:

It would take a very long time for a population resulting from a race mixture to become a fairly homogeneous group, and in the meantime it might suffer from the embarrassment of a considerable portion of poor grade humanity.[16]

The greatest danger was that the 'advanced races' would be diluted as a result of widespread miscegenation, with deleterious effects on the whole of humanity. The distinguished British botanist R. Ruggles-Gates wrote a powerful book warning about crosses between 'an advanced and primitive stock', which was undesirable from every point of view, producing individuals who were 'socially maladjusted and physically disharmonious'. The racial elements of the more primitive stock would dilute and weaken the 'better element of the more progressive stock, with a retarding or degrading effect on the progressive stock as a whole'.[17]

Distorted images of mestizo Latin America were constantly used as a warning and admonition of what would happen as a result of extensive and prolonged miscegenation. In his Robert Boyle lecture for 1919, Sir Arthur Keith spoke of the sense of racial caste that had historically preserved the white race. The Spanish and Portuguese had broken down the barriers that nature had set up between them and the Indian peoples. The consequences, he believed, were only too apparent. The whole of Latin America had given the world 'a jangling series of small peoples', not any one of them equal in body or mind to the pioneer Iberian stock.[18] William McDougall wrote with palpable alarm about the future prospects of widespread racial fusion when intermarriage of the most diverse stocks would have taken place on a vast scale, so that, after the lapse of a century of such mingled existence, miscegenation would be far advanced, or perhaps, completed; and the remnant of the peoples that have built up our modern civilization would have been absorbed in the general mass, like a few drops of milk in a basin of coffee, leaving upon the mass hardly any recognisable trace of their racial qualities.[19]

Many Americans felt that the future apprehended by McDougall was already upon them. Their fears were formed and intensified by the intelligence tests carried out during 1916 and 1917 on 1.7 million recruits to the army that appeared to produce quite predictable results, confirming what practically every other form of measurement had suggested during the previous hundred years. The Nordic race was intellectually superior to southern and eastern Europeans and they, in turn, were more able than the Afro-Americans and mulattoes. Intelligence testing of American children suggested a rise in intelligence as the proportion of white blood increased. Full-blood Afro-Americans were assessed at 64 per cent of Europeans, half-castes at 70 per cent, quadroons at 96 per cent.[20] When this material was correlated with the census data showing an increase of racial mixture, anxieties spiralled. In his 1923 book A Study of American Intelligence, C.C. Brigham pointed to the increasing proportion of mulattoes to every 1000 Afro-Americans enumerated at each census, from 126 in 1850 to 136 in 1870, to 179 in 1890 and 264 in 1910. 'We must face the possibility', he wrote, 'of racial admixture here that is infinitely worse than that faced by any European country today'. The United States was 'incorporating the Negro into our racial stock', while all of Europe was comparatively free from this taint. The collateral damage was already apparent. All the evidence available suggested that American intelligence was declining because the general results of the 'admixture of higher and lower orders of intelligence must inevitably be a mean between the two'.[21]

One of the reputed characteristics of mixed-blood people was their dissatisfaction with their own circumstances and a resulting penchant for political activism. Agitation was thereby linked with crime and dissolute behaviour in the commentator's prescription of mulatto shortcomings. Professor A. Carr-Saunders, the distinguished British geneticist, observed in 1922 that the mulatto was not of one race or the other. He was an outcast who grew up with neither the 'pride of the white man' nor the feeling of community experienced by his coloured relatives, whose position with regard to other races was generally accepted as something inevitable.[22] The story of the malcontented mixed blood served a number of related purposes. It suggested that anti-colonial activity in overseas colonies and agitation against segregation in the United States were both unnecessary and unnatural, stemming from the individual psychological problems of the mulatto. There was the additional small vanity that it was the white blood that clamoured for freedom. The genuine native – or the full-blooded Afro-American – showed no indication of wanting to take action against the status quo. Edward East declared in 1923 that only when there was white blood in his veins did the 'Negro or the Malaysian cry out against the supposed injustice of his condition'.[23]

In his book *Democracy and Race Friction*, J. M. Mecklin remarked that it was only natural that it was from mulattoes that the most vigorous protests arose against racial discrimination. They lived in an atmosphere that was not 'psychologically healthful'. It was an atmosphere of protest. The 'Negro of pure blood', on the other hand, did not lie awake at night brooding over the loss of human rights.[24] The prominent sociologist E. B. Reuter was more sympathetic to the Afro-American but believed that America's race problem was 'the problem of the mulatto'. It was this discontented and psychologically unstable group that gave rise to the acute phases of the 'so-called race problem'.[25] While visiting the United States in 1924, the distinguished British scientist Julian Huxley came to the conclusion that the growing admixture of races had enormously aggravated the problem, referring to the

> undoubted fact that by putting some of the white man's mind into the mulatto you not only make him more capable and more ambitious . . . but you increase his discontent and create an obvious injustice if you continue to treat him like any full blooded African. The American Negro is making trouble because of the American white blood that is in him.[26]

G. F. Lane-Fox Pitt-Rivers was another Englishman with a distinguished name (or should it be names?) who would have disagreed with Julian Huxley on many of the issues of the age. But on mulattoes they were as one, with Pitt-Rivers writing in 1927 that '[i]t is the mixed bloods, Negroes and Kaffirs with white blood in their veins, who led the revolt against the white man's influence'.[27]

While one British scientist with an illustrious name was visiting America and thinking about what he termed 'the Negro problem', another one was writing to the leaders of the Empire-Commonwealth, advising them about similar questions in the British Dominions and colonial possessions. Major Leonard Darwin wrote to the prime ministers assembled at the Imperial Conference in London in 1923, warning them about the dangers of miscegenation – that interbreeding between widely divergent races was likely to result in the production of types 'inferior to both parent stocks'. This was the view of distinguished scientists and also a 'common belief among his countrymen'.[28]

Hostility to miscegenation was much more pronounced in the United States and reached a peak of intensity in the early twentieth century. In 1931 twenty-nine of the forty-eight states prohibited the intermarriage of whites with Afro-Americans or with individuals of other races. Many of these laws remained on the statute books until they were declared unconstitutional by the Supreme Court in 1967. E. B. Reuter observed that although in 1931 some states lacked such legislation, this should not be taken as evidence that such marriages were approved or even that there was popular indifference to them. In fact, the strength of public opposition to them exercised effective control even without relevant legislation. Reuter was told by a senior government official in Massachusetts that interracial marriages in his State were rare 'chiefly because of the violent opposition of the public towards such marriages'.[29] Ten years later the Swedish sociologist Gunar Myrdal found that white opposition to intermarriage was almost universal; it was held 'commonly, absolutely, and intensely'. Even liberal-minded northerners 'of cosmopolitan culture' in nine cases out of ten expressed a definite feeling against amalgamation. Such a person, Myrdal thought, would not be willing usually to hinder intermarriage by law. Individual liberty is to him a higher principle and, what is more important, he actually invokes it. But he will regret the exceptional cases that occur. He may sometimes hold a philosophical view that in centuries to come amalgamation is bound to happen and might become the solution. But he will be inclined to look on it as an inevitable deterioration. [30]

In six southern states – Alabama, Florida, Mississippi, North and South Carolina and Tennessee – the prohibition was embedded in the constitution. The Alabama document declared that the legislature could 'never pass any law to authorize or legalize any marriage between any white person and a Negro, or a descendant of a Negro'. It didn't matter how remote the black ancestor or how small the percentage of Afro-American blood. Entering any such marriage was a crime for which either party must be imprisoned for not less than two or not more than seven years. Some states included other races in their prohibited category. The relevant Arizona statute determined that marriage of 'persons of Caucasian blood' or their descendants with Negroes, Mongolians or Indians or their descendants would be null and void. The constitution of Florida declared that all marriages between a white person and a person of Negro descent 'to the fourth generation' were forever prohibited. Violators of the prohibition could be imprisoned for up to ten years. Any official issuing a marriage licence for an illegal union could be heavily fined and imprisoned for up to two years. A clergyman or priest officiating at such a ceremony could be imprisoned for up to a year.

A law enacted in Georgia in 1921 prohibited the marriage of a white person and a partner with any ascertainable trace of 'African, West Indian, Asiatic Indian or Mongolian blood'. Georgia, like Virginia, defined who was or was not a white person, declaring that the term should include 'only persons of the white or Caucasian race' who had no ascertainable trace of either 'Negro, African, West Indian, Asiatic Indian, Mongolian, Japanese or Chinese blood in their veins'.[31]

Myrdal may have found that his handful of intellectual liberals felt an 'irrational emotional inhibition'[32] against intermarriage but many scholars provided a powerful intellectual defence of segregation and denunciation of 'cross-breeding'. In an article on 'Race and Marriage' in the *American Journal of Sociology* in 1910, Professor Ulysses G. Weatherley argued that resistance to intermarriage was both justified and understandable and stemmed from instinctive drives, the purpose of which was to preserve racial distinctiveness. Behind what he termed 'physical aversion to alien types' was something far more important – 'an instinctive recognition of racial standards as a social capital that must not be dissipated by surrendering racial purity'.[33] Marriage was very much more than a union of two individuals. It was not a private matter. Indeed, the doyen of American human biologists, C. B. Davenport, believed that 'proper matings' were the greatest means of permanently improving the human race and saving it from imbecility, poverty, disease, immorality and racial degeneration.[34]

Similar arguments were even more forcefully advanced by Professor J. M. Mecklin in his 1914 book *Democracy and Race Friction*, which was widely read in both the United States and Australia. In a chapter titled 'Race Prejudice' he singled out the taboo placed upon mixed marriages as a factor of fundamental importance for any understanding of race antipathy. The aversion to such unions could be traced far back into biological history – to instincts that prevented the mating of different species. This was nature's method of securing permanence of type, even before the appearance of conscious choice as a factor. Also present among savages were 'quasi-instinctive forces' that operated to perpetuate the group type and the distinctive concomitant culture. In modern society, continuity of cultural traditions depended on racial integrity. 'Continuity of culture', Mecklin argued,

> depends in a very profound sense upon the continuity of the racial type of which the culture is an expression. Race in its widest sense is, like the individual, a psychophysical unity. This continuity of race type, of course, can only be attained through control of marriage relations. In primitive society custom and taboo determine, in a partly rational way, to be sure, but with infallible certainty, the persistence of race and of culture; in modern society, however, we seem more or less at the mercy of personal whim and inclination.[35]

And that was the problem. Personal inclination and taste, aesthetic feeling and the romantic sentiment of youth all played a role in the choice of marriage partners. Fortunately unconscious, instinctive forces still operated to influence in a thousand subtle ways the entrance upon the marriage relation. Mecklin referred to the feeling of ethnic solidarity and sympathy of which the individual was often entirely unconscious as well as the cumulative effect of race traditions and customs. Operating in the opposite direction was the 'natural antipathy' that regulated the relations of all widely separated peoples, 'the sentinel which keeps watch and ward over the purity of the highly developed race'.[36]

Law and custom then gave recognition to the fact that the interests and inclinations of the parties immediately concerned should be subordinated to the larger interests of the group. Society itself, or what Mecklin termed the group mind, was distinctly aware of the fundamental importance of conserving the hereditary racial basis that was the bearer of the group culture. The social condemnation of 'the union of whites and negroes' was a manifestation of this demand that group integrity be preserved. Such an 'intermingling of blood' implied a vast deal more than the union of the two people concerned. It would inevitably bring in time a profound modification of the cultural ideals of the white race as a consequence of the transformation of the ethnic background of those ideals. The loss of this 'self-poised psychophysical entity' would be a serious disaster, threatening civilisation itself. Hence prejudice against colour in its last analysis may be prompted by 'laudable instincts of self-preservation'.[37]

There were further quite practical reasons to deter or actually prohibit interracial marriage. What Mecklin called the 'fundamental incompatibilities of racial temperament and tradition' operated to make the great majority of actual unions between the two groups unhappy and doomed to disappointment, social isolation and violence. A contemporary study of twenty-nine white women living with Afro-Americans found that twelve of the women were prostitutes, three were of criminal repute, two died by the hand of their coloured husbands, one committed suicide, one was insane, two sued for divorce, two deserted their husbands, five seemed satisfied and information 'as to the other four was not to be had'.[38]

A further reason to discountenance such marriages was the bearing of mixed-race children. For where races differed so greatly the result of the amalgamation was neither one type nor the other, but 'a confusion of the two'. The result of the blend was a mongrel. And it was no accident of history that mongrel peoples were 'almost always characterized by instability of political institutions' and a general 'inchoateness of civilization'.[39]

White American concern about intermarriage and racial mixing peaked during the first decade of the twentieth century. A *Bibliography of the Negro in Africa and America* published in 1928 listed books and articles published on the subject of 'race and mixture'. There were eight items before 1865, none from 1865 to 1885, ten from 1886 to 1900 and 108 after the turn of the century.[40] Attempts to introduce laws prohibiting intermarriage in the northern states peaked in 1913, but were still being made in the 1920s and 1930s. Writing in 1931, E.B. Reuter remarked that such attempts to extend the swag of discriminatory legislation left no reasonable doubt that general white sentiment, wherever the matter was brought to public attention, was 'almost universally opposed to mixed unions'. Running in parallel with this sentiment was the continuing assault from both popular and most expert opinion on the figure of the mulatto. This campaign was apparent in many parts of the world – in the United States, Britain, Australia and other white Dominions[41] – and racial ideology passed rapidly across national borders.

The leading authority on the history of marriage provided little encouragement to anyone considering interracial marriage in the early years of the twentieth century. Edward Westermarck's three-volume *The History of Human Marriage* was published to critical acclaim in 1891 and was still in print in 1921 when the fifth edition was published. Westermarck believed that probably every race considered it a disgrace to marry within a very different race, 'at least if it be an inferior one'. Such attitudes, he felt, were chiefly due to racial or national pride and lack of sympathy with or positive antipathy to individuals of another race. For this reason antipathy was particularly common where races greatly differed from each other in 'ideas, habits and civilization generally'.

But, beyond all of these, Westermarck believed that

> some sexual aversion akin to the instinctive feeling which deters animals of distinct species from pairing with each other is in many cases really felt against sexual intercourse with persons of a race whose appearance is very different from that of one's own, and that such aversion is particularly common in women, in whom the sexual instinct is generally more discriminatory than in men.[42]

By the time that Westermarck was persuading readers about the dangers of miscegenation, the eugenics movement was winning converts in all Western countries. We should now consider these ideas.

CHAPTER 3

Eugenics – a New Religion

Francis Galton both gave birth to and christened the eugenics movement, which attained its greatest influence in the early decades of the twentieth century. Galton combined a commitment to evolution and a deep interest in inheritance. One of his earliest books *Hereditary Genius* was about the transmission of high intellectual ability across the generations. He had an upper-class Englishman's regard for family, breeding, heritage and ancestry; a penchant for aristocracy. In his book *Natural Inheritance* he dealt with the way in which individuals inherited characteristics from parents and ancestors, and with the continuing influence of earlier generations. 'Though one half of every child may be said to be derived from either parent', he declared, it was possible to receive characteristics from a distant progenitor which neither of the parents possessed. Indeed, any parent had a 'store of hidden property' which might be manifested in their children.[1]

Galton argued that children inherited a quarter of their characteristics from each parent and one sixteenth from each grandparent.

If this scale was projected backwards, a child could potentially receive heritage from as many as 196 ancestors. 'We appear then', he observed, to be 'severally built up out of a host of minute particles of whose nature we know nothing', some of which might be derived from any one progenitor.[2] Latent characteristics could therefore emerge unexpectedly in later generations, and so a child often resembled an ancestor in some feature or character that neither of his parents personally possessed. Employing an extended metaphor, Galton wrote:

> We are told that buried seeds may be dormant for many years, so that when a plot of ground that was formerly cultivated is again deeply dug into and upturned, plants that had not been known to grow on a spot within the memory of man, will frequently make their appearance.[3]

But if Galton's concern was with ancestors and the past alone, his work would have failed to exercise the influence that it achieved among his contemporaries. While he was interested in transmission of characteristics from the past, he was even more concerned with transmission forward into the future. The value of good stock to the wellbeing of future generations was therefore obvious. Aristocracies of birth, talent or race could most easily be perpetuated if there was a 'refusal to blend freely' with inappropriate stock.[4]

An understanding of inheritance could provide the key to improving not just families but whole races. With rigorous research, freed from popular prejudice, it would be possible to judge the direction in which the different races needed to be guided. And then, by rigorous supervision of breeding, the race could be improved. Even the evolution of a higher humanity might be furthered, with Galton arguing that

> [t]he most merciful form of what I venture to call 'eugenics' would consist in watching for the indications of superior strains of races, and in so favouring them that their progeny shall outnumber and gradually replace that of the old one.[5]

An understanding of evolution – of the direction in which humanity had advanced and how this had occurred – could be applied to the problem of what its destiny might be. If contemporaries wished to assist in 'the order of events' they could do so by furthering the course of evolution.[6] Galton explained in his book *Inquiries into Human Faculty* of 1883 that his general object had been to take note of the 'varied hereditary faculties' of different men, families and races. This was done in order to learn how far history had shown 'the practicability of supplanting inefficient human stock by better strains' and thus furthering the ends of evolution 'more rapidly and with less distress than if events were left to their own course'.[7]

In later papers and lectures Galton more precisely defined what he meant by eugenics – the purpose of which was to attend to the 'improvement of our stock'. It was the science that dealt with all the influences that improved the 'inborn qualities of a race' and developed them to the utmost advantage.[8] To Galton there was a pressing necessity to establish the national importance of eugenics. While addressing a prestigious audience at a meeting of London's Sociological Society in 1904, he declared that eugenics must be introduced into the national conscience, like a new religion. It has, indeed, strong claims to become an orthodox religious tenet of the future, for eugenics co-operate with the workings of nature by securing that humanity shall be represented by the fittest races. What nature does blindly, slowly, and ruthlessly, man may do providently, quickly and kindly. As it lies within his power, so it becomes his duty to work in that direction. The improvement of our stock seems to me one of the highest objects that we can reasonably attempt.[9]

Galton held out before his audience the prospect of a eugenically moulded society of the future. The general tone of domestic, social and political life would be higher. The whole race would be less foolish, less frivolous, less excitable and more politically provident. Men of an order of ability very rare in contemporary society would 'become more frequent'. Britain would be better fitted to fulfil her 'vast imperial opportunities'.[10]

The discussion in London that followed Galton's paper was led by Professor Karl Pearson, a distinguished mathematician and polemicist. Pearson became one of the foremost advocates for eugenics over the following twenty years from his base at London University. Among the complimentary remarks addressed to his elderly mentor, he urged upon his audience the hope that the whole doctrine of descent, of inheritance and of selection of the fittest would become a part of everyday life, of social customs and of conduct. This was, he declared, 'the gravest problem which lies before the Caucasian races'.[11] Pearson's sense of urgency came from what might be called temporal anxiety. Everything appeared to be open to change, to the driving currents of evolution. Nothing was permanent; nothing could be taken for granted. 'The Darwinian revelation', he observed, showed that humanity could no longer be considered static. 'We know it to be kinetic', he continued, 'the races of which it is composed being in a perpetual state of change'. It was to the future that the scholar and the statesman had to look and, above all, to the prospects for the race. The judgement of history, the sagacity and achievements of contemporary leaders, would turn henceforth on the measure of their contribution to the 'racial progress of their nations in the generations which succeed them'.[12] Eugenics in Pearson's definition was the study of agencies under social control that were able to improve or impair the racial qualities of future generations, either physically or mentally.[13]

Benjamin Kidd was another prominent writer who listened to Francis Galton on that spring afternoon in 1904. Ten years earlier, his book *Social Evolution* had achieved spectacular success. It first appeared in January 1894 and was reprinted eight times by the end of the year and twice more in the first six months of 1895. It was quickly translated into nine languages. Like Pearson, Kidd was a child of Darwin's revolution, the significance of which he thought was 'without parallel in the history of thought'. He too felt the imperative need to face the future. Social and political endeavour, he argued, had to be concerned with that 'silent majority which is always in the future'.[14]

William McDougall agreed with this assessment, believing that political ideas must be evaluated not just in relation to their impact on contemporaries. Rather, they should be judged also by reference to 'the lives of generations yet unborn'.[15] And the future could not be left to unfold as it might. Danger beckoned everywhere. In a series of lectures to the Royal College of Physicians in March 1894, Professor J. B. Haycraft warned of the need to preserve the character of the race from deterioration. No other obligation was as important because the 'most fundamental good' that could be achieved was that which would 'add to the organic excellence of the race'.[16]

But danger was to be expected because struggle and competition was at the very centre of the evolutionary system; it was the inescapable, relentless mainspring of change. 'With whatever feelings we may regard the conflict', Benjamin Kidd wrote, it was necessary to remember that it was 'the first condition of progress'.[17]

Karl Pearson was even more tough-minded about the need to accept the inevitability of conflict and of interracial struggle that produced intense suffering while it was in progress:

> [T]he struggle and that suffering have been the stages by which the white man has reached his present stage of development . . . This dependence on progress of the survival of the fitter race, terribly black as it may seem . . . gives the struggle for existence its redeeming features; it is the fiery crucible out of which comes the finer metal.[18]

When Darwin had written about social conflict in *The Descent of Man* he had referred to the struggle of individuals within society, and this was a common view during the 1870s and 1880s. But by the turn of the century, in an atmosphere of intensified commercial and colonial rivalry, the emphasis turned to competition between races and nations. For Karl Pearson the nation was an 'organized whole' in continual struggle with other nations, either by force of arms or by trade and economic processes.[19] 'The struggle of man against man', he declared,

> with its victory to the tougher and more crafty: the struggle of tribe against tribe, with its defeat for the less socially organized; the contest of nation with nation whether in trade or war, with the mastery for the foreseeing nation, for the nation with the cleaner bill of health, the more united purpose of its classes, and the sounder intellectual equipment of its units: are not these only phases of the struggle for existence?[20]

Race continued to occupy a dominant position in the intense discussion of the early twentieth century about inheritance, competition, degeneration and survival. Miscegenation was regarded as one of the greatest dangers faced by any society – more so for white, advanced nations because there was so much more to lose. If anything, the mulatto was more dangerous than the criminal, the prostitute, the drunkard or the feeble-minded. Such anxieties were more apparent in the United States with its large Afro-American population already agitating against the rigid controls of segregation. E. G. Conklin, the Professor of Biology at Princeton, believed that the greatest danger that faced any 'superior race' was that of 'amalgamation with inferior stock and the consequent lowering of inherited capacities'. And while he thought that in the distant future there would be a mingling of races, every consideration should lead those who believed in the superiority of the white race to strive to 'preserve its purity and to establish and maintain the segregation of the races', for the longer this was maintained the greater the predominance of the white race would be.[21]

Racial preservation was so important that it must necessarily involve restrictions on individual freedom. Conklin believed that among all organisms the race or species was of paramount importance. Race preservation, not self-preservation, was the first law of nature. And the improvement of the race must take precedence over other causes. In fact, individual freedom should be subordinated to racial welfare. The individual's physical and intellectual development must not interfere with his racial and ethical obligations. 'We shall rise', Conklin asserted, 'only as the race rises'.[22]

Eugenics was about more than ideas. It embodied an in-built blueprint for action – for the influence of what Pearson called the 'agencies under social control' to introduce practical reforms for achieving what the converts believed would be the betterment of the race. The eugenicists wanted the state to take action across a wide range of fronts – encouraging the fit and intelligent to marry early and to have more children; to improve social conditions for mothers and infants; and, more controversially, to prevent those regarded as 'undesirables' from breeding, even by sterilisation when necessary. This agenda was influential in many countries in the early years of the twentieth century, although the success of the eugenics movement varied greatly from place to place.

The biological scientists, ethnographers and social reformers who took up the cause were also concerned with international politics. There was an inevitability about this. The competition and conflict they thought inherent in the process of natural selection did not cease at national borders. Indeed, its most significant arena was the global one. Race was inescapably an international issue, as were miscegenation and the problems created by unprecedented global mobility. Racial issues in the United States, South Africa, Australia and India were widely reported in newspapers all around the world. The mestizo countries of central and south America and the Caribbean elicited intense interest and frequent condemnation from commentators in northern Europe and the United States. Segregation in America and South Africa and immigration restrictions in California, Australia and New Zealand were widely reported and discussed and were regarded as policies of international significance. So too were the beginnings of anti-colonial agitation in places as widely separated as India, Egypt, Indochina and Indonesia. Nascent third-world nationalism was frequently seen in terms of racial conflict and having a cohesion and unity of purpose that was never there.

One of the most influential discussions of international racial issues of the early twentieth century was the Romanes Lecture of 1902, delivered by James Bryce, entitled 'The Relations Between the Advanced and the Backward Races of Mankind'. Bryce was one of the most cosmopolitan and widely travelled scholars in the English-speaking world. Much of his writing embodied a global perspective. He appreciated that the steamship, the telegraph and the spread of European imperial authority had brought the peoples of the world into unprecedented intimacy. One of the greatest achievements of modern science had been to make the world small, with the result that the fortunes of every race and state had become 'involved with those of any other'. The unprecedented closeness of contact – 'so much closer and more widespread than ever in the past' – had created an utterly unique situation.[23] In fact, Bryce believed it was 'a crisis in the history of the world' that would profoundly affect the destiny of mankind.[24] As Europe had extended its trade and sovereignty to every corner of the globe, the danger of miscegenation grew in direct proportion to the increased inter-action. But Bryce was a man of his time, and was convinced that the mixture of Europeans with Afro-Americans or Hindus 'seldom showed good results'. The typical offspring was apt to be physically inferior to both parent stocks, and probably 'more beneath the aver-age mental level of the superior than above the mental level of the inferior'.[25] For Bryce this was a problem of universal importance. He declared that for the future of mankind,

> nothing is more vital than that some races should be maintained at the highest level of efficiency, because the work they can do for thought and art and letters, for scientific discovery and for raising the standard of conduct, will determine the general progress of humanity. If therefore we were to suppose the blood of the races which are now most advanced were to be diluted, so to speak, by that of those most backward, not only would more be lost to the former than would be gained to the latter, but there would be a loss, possibly an irreparable loss, to the world at large.[26]

Bryce's lecture, and particularly this passage, was quoted over and over again in literature about race during the next twenty-five years. It was seen as a masterly summing-up of the argument against 'indiscriminate surrender of race purity'.[27] Bryce confronted the dilemma of reconciling increasingly intimate relations between the races of the world and the inherent dangers in miscegenation.

As one of his American admirers phrased it, the problem was to facilitate cooperation in the work of civilisation without the 'mongrelization of the world's people'.[28]

Another global problem that exercised Bryce was the future of living space for the Europeans for what he called the 'leading and ruling races of the world'. Like most of his contemporaries, he considered the tropics unsuitable for permanent white settlement. They could be left out of the question. Only the temperate zone appeared to offer a haven for colonists of the future. But the whole area was rapidly filling up and would in a very short time be unable to receive any more migrants from Europe. The world seemed to be entering a new era, one that Bryce feared would result in increased tension and conflict.[29]

This theme was taken up by the Australian scholar/politician C. H. Pearson and developed further in his highly influential book *National Life and Character*, published in 1894. Pearson subtitled his book 'A Forecast'. In it he anticipated the time when the white race would be penned in by invisible biological barriers while the prolific black, brown and yellow peoples would increase in the tropical regions. The day would come, he warned, and perhaps not a far distant one, when the European observer would look around to see the globe 'girdled with a continuous zone of black and yellow races no longer too weak for aggression or under tutelage' but independent in government, monopolising the trade of their own regions and 'circumscribing the industry of the Europeans'. Chinamen, Indians and Africans would be invited to international conferences, and welcomed as allies in the quarrels of the civilised world. The citizens of these countries would then

> be taken up into the social relations of the white races, will throng
> the English turf, or the salons of Paris, and will be admitted to
> intermarriage . . . We shall wake to find ourselves elbowed and
> hustled, and perhaps even thrust aside, by peoples whom we
> looked down upon as servile and thought of as bound always to
> minister to our needs.

Pearson observed that it would be idle to say that, if his forecast should come to pass, 'our pride of place will not be humiliated'.[30]

Pearson died soon after his book was published. He did not live to appreciate the prescience of his forecast or the large number of books produced over the next thirty years that picked up on his warning about the possible eclipse of the white race, books with titles like *The Menace of Colour, The Clashing Tides of Colour* and *The Rising Tide of Colour*. One of the most powerful of the genre was B.L. Putman Weale's *The Conflict of Colour*, published in 1910 and subtitled 'Being a Detailed Examination of Racial Problems throughout the World with Special Reference to the English-speaking Peoples'. Weale considered the question of whether the Europeans could continue to dominate Asia and Africa. He foresaw the rise of nationalism and the ultimate demand for independence. 'The day is fast approaching', he wrote, 'when all men will be not only free but independent'. Those who refused to see this and trusted to temporising measures behind which lurked the shadow of force were 'the real enemies of their country, and not the patriots, the imperialists, they so constantly proclaim themselves'.[31]

For England, questions of race were of supreme importance and every day that passed added to their urgency. 'These questions of Asia, of Africa', he observed, 'with their teeming races, have paramount importance, in a way that was never the case before'.[32]

In America similar foreboding was apparent but directed inward rather than projected outward to a vast and restive empire. In December 1907 the members of the American Sociological Society heard and then discussed a paper with the title 'Is Race Friction Between Blacks and Whites in the United States Growing and Inevitable?' The speaker, A. M. Stone, observed that black Americans were slowly developing a sense of their own racial solidarity, their own distinctive voice, and through books, papers and social organisations were both 'giving utterance to its discontent and making known its demands'. And with this

dawning consciousness of race there is likewise coming an appreciation of the limitations and restrictions which hem in its unfolding and development. One of the best indices to the possibilities of increased racial friction is the negro's own recognition of the universality of the white man's racial antipathy towards him. This is the one clear note above the storm of protest against the things that are, that in his highest aspirations everywhere the white man's 'prejudice' blocks the colored man's path. And the white man may with possible profit pause long enough to ask the deeper significance of the negro's finding of himself. May it not be part of a general awakening of the darker races of the earth.[33]

The discussant who contributed the most detailed response to the lecture was the Afro-American radical intellectual W. E. B. du Bois. He warned his readers that if the southern whites hoped that

the blacks were not going to demand equal rights and fair treatment, then they were certain to be disappointed. He referred to a
growing protest movement that was not confined to the north, to
a few leaders or to the mulattoes. 'Daily and yearly it is growing', he
declared, and it was that development that had created the so-
called 'Negro problem'. If the white south was planted immovably
on the proposition that most human beings were to be kept

> in absolute and unchangeable serfdom and inferiority to the
> Teutonic world and if we assume that not only the Negroes of
> America, but those of Africa and the West Indies – not only
> Negroes, but Indians, Malays, Chinese and Japanese, not to men-
> tion the Mediterranean lands – are determined to contest this
> absurd stand to the death, then the world has got some brisk days
> ahead, and race frictions will inevitably grow not only in the United
> States but the world over.[34]

The publication of books relating to racial conflict increased
in the 1920s as Europe endeavoured to recover from the damage
to its power and prestige exacted by World War I. Tens of thousands of Africans and Indians had been brought to Europe to
assist in the war effort. President Wilson's declarations about
self-determination encouraged nationalists all over the world;
weakened Imperial powers faced increasing agitation in their
far-flung colonies. In his book *Ethnos or the Problem of Race Considered from a New Point of View*, Sir Arthur Keith observed that
the differentiation of humanity into races was a source of continuous trouble to mankind. Every morning when he opened his
newspaper he found that peace in some part of the world was being

disturbed by the friction engendered 'where race meets race'.[35] G. H. L. Pitt-Rivers thought that in every direction the world was confronted by the clash and struggle for supremacy between races, by the problems created by races that failed to become 'reconciled or contented under European control'. There was, indeed, a worldwide phenomenon of 'recalcitrant and irreconcilable black races'.[36] In his book *The Menace of Colour*, J. W. Gregory, like James Bryce before him, referred to the 'narrowing of the world' that had created 'increasing difficulty in the relations between the different races of mankind'. We are warned, he remarked, that civilisation is endangered by the rising tide of colour, and the progress of humanity by 'the rising tide of colour prejudice'.[37]

Both Pitt-Rivers and Gregory referred to one of the most popular and alarmist books of the genre, Lothrop Stoddard's *The Rising Tide of Colour Against White World Supremacy*, published in 1920. In outlining the genesis of his book, Stoddard explained that more than a decade earlier he had become convinced that 'momentous modifications' of existing race relations were impending, that the keynote of twentieth-century world politics would be the relations between the primary races of mankind.[38] In a chapter entitled 'The Crisis of the Ages' he declared: 'Ours is a solemn moment. We stand at a crisis – the supreme crisis of the ages'.[39] The white race was beset on all sides – by economic competition, by migration of 'lower human types', by demographic failure at home. Nowhere, he argued,

can the white man endure coloured competition; everywhere the 'East can *underlive* the West'. The grim truth of the matter is this:

The whole white race is exposed, immediately and ultimately, to the possibility of social sterilization and final replacement or absorption by the teeming coloured races.[40]

Eugenics, the 'new biological revelation', would save the day. The overwhelming importance of heredity and the supreme value of 'superior stocks' would become more generally understood. A true race consciousness would bridge political gulfs, remedy social abuses and exorcise the 'lurking spectre of miscegenation'.[41]

Though much of the scientific and scholarly attention was directed to people of mixed descent, there was also a large literature on the Australian Aborigines. We should now consider this material before returning to Australia itself.

CHAPTER 4

The Most Primitive

of Man

It was a coincidence that the emergence of scientific racism in the late eighteenth century coincided with the British occupation of Australia. Reports about the Aborigines could be immediately employed in constructing theories about race, human equality and the origins of human society. They continued to be so used through the nineteenth century. As early as 1774 James Burnett referred to accounts he had read of Cook's expedition of four years earlier in his book *Of the Origin and Progress of Language*. He explained that he had been informed by travellers who had lately been in Australia that the huts of the New Hollanders were 'not near so well built as those of the beavers'. And while they had the use of speech, Burnett could 'hardly believe' that they had invented it.[1]

A generation later, William Lawrence referred to the Aborigines while drawing attention to the 'differences which exist between inhabitants of the different regions of the globe'. Compare, he urged, the highly civilised nations of Europe to a 'troop of naked, shivering and starved New Hollanders', a horde of filthy Hottentots 'or the whole of the more or less barbarous tribes that cover the entire continent of Africa'.[2] The distinction of colour between white and black was not more striking

> than the pre-eminence of the former in moral feelings and mental endowments . . . The latter . . . indulge, almost universally, in disgusting debauchery and sensuality, and display gross selfishness, indifference to the pains and pleasures of others, insensibility to beauty of form, order and harmony, and an almost entire want of what we comprehend altogether under the expression of elevated sentiments, manly virtues and moral feeling. The hideous savages of Van Diemen's Land, of New Holland, New Guinea, and some neighbouring islands, the Negroes of Congo and some other parts exhibit the most disgusting moral as well as physical portrait of man.[3]

Though deeply divided on matters that, at the time, appeared to be of fundamental importance, the monogenesists and polygenesists could agree about the savagery of Africans and Oceanic Negroes, as Aborigines and Melanesians were often known. De Gobineau remarked that Oceania had the special privilege of providing the 'most ugly, degraded and repulsive specimens of the race' that seemed to have been created to provide a link between man and the brute, pure and simple.[4] J. C. Prichard was only a little more flattering in his description of nations that had never emerged from the savage state:

Such are all the Savages scattered through the distant Islands of the Southern hemisphere. Wherever we find the people naked, destitute barbarians running wild in the woods, there we also observe them to be black, and to partake considerably of the Negro form and character.[5]

A key assumption underlying ethnographic speculation at the time of Australia's founding settlements was that of a great chain of being. In his *An Account of the Regular Gradation in Man* of 1799, Charles White observed that everyone who had studied natural history must have been led to 'contemplate the beautiful gradation that subsists among created beings' from the highest to the lowest. From man down to the smallest creatures, nature exhibited 'to our view an immense chain of beings, endued with various degrees of intelligence and active powers, suitable to their stations in the general system'.[6] As well as grading all living creatures, White took the further and critically important step of arranging human races in hierarchical order. In a section entitled 'On the Graduation in Man' he argued that man differed more from man than man from beast and that there seemed to be a difference 'in the original capacity of the different tribes of mankind'.[7] Africans were in every way closer to monkeys than other people. In whatever way they differed from the European, 'the particularity brings him nearer to the ape'.[8]

White referred to the recent work of the Dutch anatomist Peter Camper, who was one of the first scientists to try to provide means of measuring skulls in order to establish clear and demonstrable racial differences. He chose the slope of the forehead, or facial angle, as the means by which to pursue his research findings. He explained that from the moment he acquired two African skulls he desired 'nothing so much as to compare these two heads with that of a European, and to unite them with the head of a monkey'. He discovered that a line drawn from the forehead to the upper lip demonstrated the difference between the faces of different nations and the resemblance 'betwixt the head of a Negro and that of a monkey'.[9] Camper recorded his assessment of facial angles – Greek antique statues were the standard of measure, recording 100°, Europeans came in at 80°–90°; Asiatics 75°–80°; American Indians 70°–75°; Africans 60°–70°; orang-outangs 50°–60°; and common monkeys 40°–50°. In summing up the substance of his book, White reached the following conclusions:

1. There were material differences in the physical organization of various classes of mankind.

2. Taking the European man as a standard of comparison, on the one hand and the monkey tribes on the other, and, comparing the classes of mankind with the standards, and with each other, they may be so arranged as to form a pretty regular gradation in respect to the differences in the bodily structure and economy, the European standing at the head, as being farthest removed from the brute creation.[10]

Camper's attempt to assess facial angles in order to distinguish racial difference pioneered over a hundred years of endeavour to measure the configuration and volume of skulls and then the weight, size and structure of the brain, using increasingly more sophisticated techniques and equipment. But regardless of the method or means of measurement, the result was almost always the same. The Europeans came in on top of the table, with Africans and Aborigines at the bottom with smaller skulls, smaller, less complicated brains, skulls that were the wrong shape or judged to be primitive in formation.

The simplest technique of measurement was to determine the cubic capacity of the skull by blocking all the holes but one, then pouring lead shot into the cavity and finally finding the amount of water displaced by the shot. This was the method used by American Samuel Morton who, during the first half of the nineteenth century, amassed a collection of 840 skulls of 'various races and families of man'. He published tables recording the cubic capacity of skulls of the races in question:

Teutonic	92 inches
Malay	85 inches
African	83 inches
Mongolian	82 inches
Australian	75 inches[11]

Commenting on Morton's tables, J. C. Nott observed that the Aborigines (or 'Oceanic Negroes') had similar skulls to Africans, displaying like them narrow, elongated heads, defective foreheads, small internal capacity and projecting jaws. They represented the lowest grade in the human family. In fact,

their anatomical characteristics are certainly very remarkable. While in countenance they present an extreme of the prognathous type hardly above that of the orang-outang, they possess at the same time the smallest brains of the whole of mankind, being in accordance with Morton's measurements, 17 cubic inches less than the brain of the Teutonic race.[12]

Phrenology was one of the offshoots from the ongoing study of skulls and brains. Founded by the German doctor F. J. Gall, it was popularised in the English-speaking world by George Combe's books *Elements of Phrenology* of 1824 and *The Constitution of Man* published in 1828. Phrenology was developed into an elaborate intellectual system built on the twin assumptions that specific areas of the brain governed particular moral characteristics and intellectual qualities and that the configuration of the skull corresponded exactly with the shape of the brain, which was clearly divided into specific 'organs'. The professional phrenologist could therefore read off the character of individuals – and of whole racial groups – by closely examining the skull.

Given the avid collection of Aboriginal skulls and their distribution to institutions and private collectors in Europe and North America, most phrenologists aspired to having at least one of their own. Combe observed in 1828 that every phrenologist knew that the Australians and 'other savage tribes' were distinguished by great deficiencies in their moral and intellectual organisation. It was a fact 'demonstrated by specimens in most Phrenological Collections'.[13] The natives of America and New Holland could not with their present brains adopt European civilisations. The contemporary reader could find specimens of their skulls in the phrenological collections and on comparing them with those of Europeans would find that in the former the 'organs' relating to intellect, benevolence and conscientiousness were 'greatly inferior in size'.[14]

Anatomists working outside the framework of phrenology arrived at similar conclusions about the Australians. For the French scientist Paul Broca they were inferior to all the other races that had come into permanent contact with Europeans.[15] His colleague Paul Topinard determined that Aborigines had the smallest brains of any known race.[16] In an influential work that summarised a generation of anatomical research, Carl Vogt observed that there was

> an almost regular series in the cranial capacity of such nations and races, as since historical times, have taken little or no part in civilization. Australians, Hottentots and Polynesians, nations in the lowest state of barbarism, commence the series, and no one can deny that the place they occupy in relation to cranial capacity and cerebral weight corresponds with the degree of their intellectual capacity and civilization.[17]

With the rising influence of evolutionary ideas in the second half of the nineteenth century, European views of Aboriginal people both changed and remained the same. Much of the work of the anatomists was simply adopted and built into the new Darwinian world view. Darwin's key collaborator and publicist, T. H. Huxley, used the pre-existing measurement of skulls to illustrate man's place in nature in an important paper in 1863. He compared Aboriginal skulls with those of assorted apes and concluded that men differ more from one another than they do from their simian cousins.[18] The difference in the weight of brain between the highest and the lowest man was far greater 'both relatively and absolutely than between the lowest man and the highest ape'.[19] Thus while ethnography entered its Darwinian phase, the vilification of Africans and 'Oceanic Negroes' continued.

However, these peoples' inferiority was now assumed to arise not from their position on the Great Chain of Being but from the circumstances of being more primitive and having stood still while other races had evolved. But this very primitiveness sparked intense interest among generations of ethnographers and anthropologists. The so-called primitive tribes represented the earliest stages of evolution. They were interesting and scientifically important human fossils. In his influential book of 1865, *Primitive Culture*, Edward Tylor stated that

> [t]he thesis which I venture to sustain, within limits, is simply this, that the savage state in some measure represents an early condition of mankind, out of which the higher culture has gradually been developed or evolved, by processes still in regular operation as of old.[20]

European man could find among the Greenlanders, Maoris and other savage tribes many a trait for 'reconstructing the picture of his own primitive ancestors'.[21] Such people were hundreds of generations behind the advanced societies of the world for if the advance of culture 'be regarded as taking place along one general line' then existing savage tribes stood 'directly intermediate between animal and civilized life'.[22]

Another comparison common in nineteenth-century ethnography was that between savages and children. Each lacked discipline, was impulsive, responded to life emotionally rather than rationally, and Tylor thought it quite appropriate to apply the 'oft repeated comparison of savages to children'.[23] The corollary arrived at in many parts of the world was that savages responded best to physical punishment and that sparing the rod spoiled them as surely as it did European and American children of the Victorian era. Another widespread European belief was that children of 'lower races' were able to benefit from education when they were young but that they reached a point in early adolescence when they could make no further progress, no matter how hard their teachers worked at the task. In his 1881 book *Anthropology*, Tylor suggested that a good test when measuring the minds of lower races was to determine how far their children were able to respond to civilised education. He reported that teachers with relevant experience found that their primitive charges often learnt as well as white children to about twelve years of age but that they then 'fell off', and were left behind by 'children of the ruling race'. Tylor believed that this information fitted in well with what the anatomists were telling the world about retarded development in the brain of the Australian and the African.[24]

A linked belief of European and American scientists and sociologists was that the primitive mind was unable to comprehend intellectual, moral or aesthetic concepts and was therefore incapable of embracing civilisation. Herbert Spencer argued that there was distinct evidence that the minds of 'the inferior races' were unable to respond to ideas of even moderate complexity. He too reported that education was possible to a certain stage followed by a slowing down, and it was not only with purely intellectual conditions that this held. He explained that it was manifest

> with what we distinguish as moral cognitions. In the Australian languages there are no words answering to justice, sin, guilt. Among various of the lower races, acts of generosity or mercy are utterly incomprehensible. That is to say, the more complex relations of human action in its social bearings, are not cognisable.[25]

Evolution was about change and about developments that had taken place over vast stretches of time. Humanity was thereby given a 'pedigree of prodigious length'.[26] But change was driven by conflict and struggle. They were intrinsic to the whole process of development. Darwin believed that man, like every other animal, had 'no doubt advanced to his present high condition through a struggle for existence'.[27] And the struggle must continue, for if man was 'to advance still higher, it is to be feared that he must remain subject to severe struggle'. Otherwise, advanced societies would sink into indolence.[28] But while some races were destined to advance still higher, others were doomed to die out 'at some future period'. Darwin believed that at some time, and not very distant as measured by centuries, 'the civilized races of man will almost certainly exterminate, and replace the savage man throughout the world'. The same fate awaited the apes, and so the break between man and the species nearest to him would then be wider, for it would intervene between man 'in a more civilized state . . . even than the Caucasians' and some ape as low as a baboon 'instead of as now between the Negro or Australian and the gorilla'.[29]

While the humane might lament the fate that awaited savage races like the Australians, the process by which it was under way was beyond human control. The end result was inevitable. Evolutionary progress created both winners and losers. And while it was difficult for sympathetic observers to understand the process, Darwin explained that the increase of each species and each race was constantly checked in various ways,

> so that if any new check, even a slight one, be superadded, the race will surely decrease in number; and decreasing numbers will sooner or later lead to extinction; the end, in most cases, being promptly determined by the inroads of conquering tribes.[30]

Alfred Russel Wallace, co-discoverer with Darwin of the principles of evolution, also wrote widely about the predestined fate of tribal people, which was due to the

> great law of 'the preservation of favoured races in the struggle for life', which leads to the inevitable extinction of all those low and mentally undeveloped populations with which the Europeans come in contact. The red Indian in North America and in Brazil, the Tasmanian, Australian and New Zealander in the southern hemisphere, die out, not from any one special cause, but from the inevitable effects of an unequal mental and physical struggle. The intellectual and moral, as well as the physical qualities of the European are superior, the same powers and capacities which have made him rise in a few centuries from the condition of the wandering savage with a scanty and stationary population, to his

present state of culture and advancement, with a greater average longevity, a greater average strength, and a capacity of more rapid increase enable him when in contact with the savage man, to conquer in the struggle for existence, and to increase at his expense, just as the better adapted increase at the expense of the less adapted varieties in the animal and vegetable kingdoms – just as the weeds of Europe overrun North America and Australia, extinguishing native production by the inherent vigour of their organization, and by the greater capacity for existence and multiplication.[31]

Throughout the nineteenth century and the early twentieth century the Aboriginal people featured in almost every ethnographic and anthropological theory developed in Europe and the United States. Two Australian scholars observed in 1930 that it had been 'repeated again and again that the aborigines of Australia represent the most primitive variety of man still existing'.[32] The American scientist Edward East remarked in 1923 that the Aborigines had been 'by the common consent of the civilized world, placed intellectually at the bottom of the list of existing races comprising the human family'. Indeed, they were the zero from which anthropologists and ethnographers had 'long reckoned our intellectual progress upward'.[33] In that same year the British scholar R. Ruggles-Gates declared that the 'Australian black fellow' was an 'early Palaeolithic survival . . . and wholly incapable of coping with white man's civilisation'.[34]

As a result of research carried out in western New South Wales in 1914 Charles Davenport concluded that the Australian race represented the largest surviving group of people who displayed 'many archaic characters'. He believed it was evidence that they had not 'evolved so far as most other races from the ancestral stock'.[35] The Director of Harvard's Peabody Museum, E. A. Hooton, reached much the same conclusion. He carried out forty-one distinct measurements of skeletons, skulls and bodies of apes and assorted human types. He categorised his subjects by means of a table which listed Sub-Humans, Inferior-Humans, Typical Humans and Ultra-Humans. His conclusions were predictable. Africans and Australians were both graded as inferior human types.[36]

The significance of this judgement for evolutionary thinking may not be immediately apparent. But the Aborigines had a vital role to play. They represented the benchmark from whence all progress could be measured, thereby proving the reality of evolutionary advance. They were surviving representatives of mankind as it had been everywhere in an earlier evolutionary era; their world was where the advanced races had escaped from. Progress thus demonstrated could be assumed to promise further, continuing advance for what were seen to be the leading races of mankind.

Racial extinction was also assumed and regarded as an inevitable consequence of evolution. It was proof that the system was in motion, that there were both winners and losers in the struggle for existence. And the dynamics were beyond human control, Edward East referring to the powerlessness of man to escape from one of the fundamental conditions under which his evolution was proceeding.[37] All this conflict of races, he declared, the worsting of the weaker, nonetheless effective even when it is silent and painless, the subordination or else the slow extinction of the inferior, is not a page from the past . . . it is all taking place today beneath our eyes in different parts of the world, and more particularly and characteristically within the pale of the vigorous Anglo-Saxon civilization.[38]

Because the process of struggle and extinction was inscribed in nature itself there was little that could prevent the passing of the Aborigines and other indigenous people. The process could be ameliorated but not terminated. Moralists might lament looming extinction, but no one was to blame. Employing his most magisterial tone, Francis Galton observed that there existed a sentiment, 'for the most part quite unreasonable', against the gradual extinction of an inferior race. It rested on confusion between the race and the individual 'as if the destruction of a race was equivalent to the destruction of a large number of men'. The process of extinction, Galton believed, worked slowly and silently through the greater capacity of members of the superior race to breed and survive and their 'prepotency in mixed marriages'. He concluded his argument with a hard-headed coda:

That the members of an inferior class should dislike being elbowed out of the way is another matter; but it may be somewhat brutally argued that whenever two individuals struggle for a single place, one must yield and that there will be no more unhappiness on the whole, if the inferior yield to the superior than conversely, whereas the world will be permanently enriched by the success of the superior.[39]

For observers investigating Australia from Europe and America in the early twentieth century, the continent was in the last stages of a grand evolutionary drama in which the most primitive and the most advanced races were pitted against each other in a one-sided struggle for control of the landmass.

This part of the book has addressed a number of questions, among which was why there was such vehement hostility in Western Europe and its new-world off-shoots to miscegenation and to the resulting mixed-descent children. To provide an adequate answer it was necessary to refer to many scientists and scholars – experts at the time – and to explain the source and momentum of their ideas. While people of mixed descent could count on a dissident or an eccentric champion or two, the consensus among the scholars was almost invincible.

Humanity was divided into distinct races. They were thought to be arranged hierarchically with the white northern Europeans and their new-world cousins at the head of the class, with the rest trailing away into inferiority. But by the end of the nineteenth century the Darwinian-inspired idea of competition and struggle had become a powerful orthodoxy. Racial mixture was, therefore, undesirable at best and positively dangerous at worst, threatening the strength and imperative purity of superior races. Mixed-descent people themselves were seen as, at the very least, unfortunate victims of implacable biological laws and probably dangerous misfits and malcontents. They were threatening not only as individuals but even more so as members of an ill-starred group who were unwelcome wherever they turned.

It is time now to consider how the ideas discussed up to this point played out in Australia in the second half of the nineteenth century and the first half of the twentieth century. We begin by considering the role of racial ideas at the time of Federation.

PART 2

Ideas and Policies in Nineteenth- and Early Twentieth-century Australia

CHAPTER 5

Racial Ideas at the

Time of Federation

When the first Federal Parliament discussed questions of race there was near-unanimity. Members and Senators agreed about the centrality of race. They agreed that there was a demonstrable hierarchy of races with the northwest Europeans, the Nordics or Caucasians at the top and the Africans, Melanesians and Aborigines at the bottom. But the hierarchy was not fixed. Races were in ceaseless competition and in the struggle for survival, homogeneity, or racial purity, was advantageous. Non-Europeans were threatening, not just as economic competitors, but as a source of racial contamination.

For three months in the second half of 1901, the new parliament debated two key bills relating to race – the Immigration Restriction Bill and the Pacific Island Labourers Bill. As many people will know, the first allowed the federal government to control immigration by means of a dictation test. While not appearing to be discriminatory it was widely understood – and loudly proclaimed – that the measure was designed to prohibit the entry of non-Europeans. The second bill gave the government power to deport all the Melanesians remaining in Australia in 1906. The objective of both pieces of legislation was to create a White Australia. The long debates left no doubt about that at all. The influential Queensland senator Thomas Glassey observed that Australia had determined 'for all time' that it would be preserved for the white race.[1] Alfred Deakin declared that nothing had been so powerful in creating the momentum for Federation as the desire that Australians should be one people and remain one people 'without the admixture of other races'.[2] Isaac Isaacs, the future High Court judge and Governor-General, believed that the country was engaged in a white man's war. It was a struggle for life,

> for that higher and fuller life that all progressive nations must feel and share in. It is that struggle for victory over adverse circumstances which is the pride and glory of all advancing civilizations. It is a white man's war that we must face, and I would not suffer any black or tinted man to come in and block the path of progress. I would resist to the utmost, if it were necessary, any murky stream from disturbing the current of Australian life.[3]

For men who feared murky racial streams, miscegenation was anathema. There was constant condemnation in parliament and the press of this 'contamination of our people, and this mixture of the races'. Although the numbers involved were small, Senator Glassey observed, miscegenation would become 'a danger, a menace, and a disgrace to our civilization'.[4] In the House of Representatives Richard Edwards, member for Oxley, referred to the danger of contamination and the 'great desire we have to preserve the purity of our race'. He was particularly concerned with the 'piebald youngsters', the number of half-caste children by white Australians and Aboriginal women. The subject, he declared, was indeed painful.[5] Sir John Forrest added a powerful, prestigious voice to the cause, declaring that 'we do not want any more colour in our race, at any rate of a black kind, than we have already'.[6] His knightly colleague Sir George Reid concurred, observing that 'we have fully made up our minds that the current of Australian blood shall not assume the darker hues. This is not a matter on which there is any room for discussion'.[7]

James Ronald, member for South Melbourne, joined the emphatic chorus, warning that the country should never try to blend 'a superior with an inferior race', otherwise the Australians would 'become piebald in spite of our efforts to prevent it'.[8] South Sydney's G. B. Edwards voiced similar fears, warning that the feared racial contamination would

> proceed from the lowest strata of society and filter up until it comes to the highest, permeating the whole nation. That is what we have to fear. I do not fear that my people or my friends will mix with the inferior races, but I do fear that my descendants, in the future days of the Commonwealth, may be largely contaminated with them.[9]

No one had a good word for half-castes. Those in India, the Senate was assured by Staniforth Smith, came to a premature end with little chance of reproduction and if there were any offspring they were 'always wretched and miserable'. All anthropologists, he claimed, agreed that the white Caucasian race could not mingle with 'the Mongolian, the Hindoo or the Negro'. The teachings of science were clear that it was not possible to mix with the coloured races.[10] Henry Willis, member for Dalley, informed his colleagues that

> [w]e see in the natural world that no good comes from hybridiza-
> tion, because hybrids reproduce the vices of both parents with
> the virtues of neither, and for this reason we should preserve our
> civilization intact and uncontaminated. If we admit races of
> another civilization we are likely to have a mongrel breed thor-
> oughly out of sympathy with the aspirations of people of the
> British stock.[11]

Similar sentiments were published in contemporary journals and newspapers. The Sydney *Bulletin* carried an article in September 1901 entitled 'The Native Born Undesirable' which explained to a wide readership that there was 'very real danger of an Australian-born mongrel population'. The poor half-caste came into the world 'with criminal instincts'. He was indeed a case of a being who was 'better not to be'. The 'half-caste mongrel Aus-tralian' would remain a cheap labourer until he was eliminated.[12] In the prestigious international journal *The Nineteenth Century*, the language was more restrained but the opinions were much the same. The two Australian authors, O. P. Law and W. T. Gill, declared that hybrids were degenerate in intellect and morals and they presented 'a source of constant irritation to the higher race'. The Spanish American Republics and 'certain parts of Australia' afforded melancholy proof that they reproduced the 'vices of both parents and the virtues of neither'.[13] The leader of the federal Labor Party, J. C. Watson, expressed his racial fears in the journal *United*

Australia in December 1901, observing that nature herself had 'drawn a cleavage almost coincident with colour'. There was always latent among whites a distrust and contempt towards 'men of darker hue'. Watson concluded that history taught that the inter-mingling of an inferior with a superior race dragged the latter down, often producing a class 'even lower than either of the original elements'.[14]

For other contemporaries it was not history that manifested the most powerful lessons about miscegenation but the cosmic pro-cess of evolution that had implanted in white man 'the instinct against race mixing'. The white race, a contributor to *The Bulletin* declared, had developed

> on certain lines to a position which promises, if it does not fulfil, the evolution of a higher human type, [and] has an instinctive repugnance to mixing its blood with peoples in other stages of evolution . . .
>
> The Caucasian, with his passion for liberty, for individuality, bears the banner in the van of humanity. If he were to stop to dally with races which would enervate him, or infect him with servile submissiveness, the scheme of human evolution would be frustrated. And that's why the sane, right thinking white man instinctively objects to all mixture with coloured races.[15]

Australia's sole journal of ethnography *Science of Man* preached from a similar text, editor Dr Alex Carrell explaining to his readers that much of the degeneracy found both in Australia and in other nations had arisen from the intermarriage of different races:

Insanity, intemperance, epilepsy, immorality, and delinquency, have been produced by this hybridising of diverse races, amalgamating the bad qualities of each of them. As mongrels among horses, dogs, sheep and cattle, are worse than useless, so are the mongrels among men.

All half-castes have been held in disfavour with both races from whom they have sprung, as it was perceived how much worse they were than either of their parents.[16]

In the article in *The Bulletin* entitled 'The Native Born Undesirable', a correspondent drew his readers' attention to the problem of the half-caste who could not be deported in the way projected for the Pacific Islanders. There was nowhere to send them. But there was a real danger that an 'Australian-born mongrel population' would drive the 'decent white labourer' out of the north. He predicted that in ten years' time the native-born half-caste who currently ran around Cairns with 'lanky, bare legs' would marry and a second generation of 'Australian-born mongrels' would be on the spot. The whole problem would become 'fearfully and wonderfully complicated'.[17]

Members of parliament and the public alike were deeply concerned about racial mixture in the tropical north. Readers of the Sydney *Bulletin* were warned by travelling correspondents that in Innisfail it was possible to see 'piebalds of every nationality'.[18] At Halifax the rising generation was a 'piebald medley'.[19] To his extreme disgust, a writer walking through Cairns saw a white woman accompanied by what he presumed were two half-caste children by different fathers.[20] The member for Maranoa, James

Page, read from a contemporary newspaper for the benefit of his parliamentary colleagues about the experiences of a visitor to Townsville who counted 'sixteen different complexions' in the space of three blocks. These consisted of three '[y]ellowy-brown children', a Japanese man with a black wife and two children of a 'dirty-drab colour'.[21]

Page's Queensland colleague (the member for Kennedy, Charles McDonald) read a longer and even more alarming extract from a correspondent who wrote a series of articles in the Melbourne *Age* in 1899 about the pearling industry in Broome. The writer observed:

> Through promiscuous intercourse with aboriginal women, a hybrid race is being established, in that far corner of the Continent such as the world has never witnessed. To describe some of the children to be seen in the Broome district would utterly puzzle the cleverest ethnologist. The Malay, Jap and Philipino have crossed with blacks. The union of former white men and aboriginal women have produced half-castes who, in turn, have bred from Chinese, Malays and Manila men. A half-caste may have crossed with a quadroon or octoroon and so the mixture of nationalities and hybrids continues until Mongrelia is literally the name which should be applied to the region.[22]

Something of the disgust with interracial mixing and the emerging multi-racial population in the tropical north was expressed in a poem written by 'Milky White' and published in *The Bulletin* in 1902:

My father was raised in the dens of the West

From an unknown cross with a Jap,

My mother was bred in the Camps of the East

From an English girl and a Chinese priest;

But I don't give a rap,

For I'm partly Briton, and partly Chow,

And partly the other chap

And who are my uncles and cousins and aunts

No mortal may ever tell;

But a Hindu Strain's in my blood somewhere,

And I'm certain that sugar-slave blood I bear,

And I can't dispel

A lingering thought that my birth

Was wrought in the heat of a Northern Hell

But the blood of the white keeps surging up

At the thought of a deep disgrace

And there's never a moment of peace within

For I carry the weight of my parents' sin;

And its hideous trace

Is found in the weakness of every limb

And the impish lines on my face.

Yet I am the young Australian, slow born of a sad mishap,

With hair as straight as the hair of a 'roo,

With skin half brown and with slant eyes blue;

But I don't care a rap –

For I am partly Briton and partly Chow,

And partly the other chap.[23]

Hostility to interracial marriage appears to have been almost universal at the turn of the century. An Australian marriage manual published in 1900, *Husbands: How to Select Them, How to Manage Them, How to Keep Them*, observed that a young woman aspiring to be a worthy wife and mother would never mate with a member of 'a lower race'. And while an Indian or a Chinaman was 'civilized after a fashion' they would 'no more be her husband than an Australian black'.[24] A writer in *The Bulletin* asserted in 1901 that in the mind of every healthy white Australian 'PROVIDENCE or something' had planted 'an ineradicable repugnance to associating with . . . racial inferiors, a conscience which warns us against intermarrying with them'.[25] J. C. Watson declared that those of 'our daughters and sisters' who married non-Europeans were regarded as 'self-sentenced outcasts'.[26]

A tragedy resulting from such a marriage was played out during the second half of 1900 involving Jimmy and Ethel Governor. Jimmy Governor was born in 1875 in northern New South Wales, the son of an Aboriginal woman and an Irish father. He was educated by missionaries to a standard higher than many of his white contemporaries. He could read and write and continued to read popular novels after leaving school. His work experience was typical of the rural working class – he went fencing, trapping and horse breaking. He was apparently hardworking, industrious and didn't drink. He said that he was 'never a loafer like some black fellows' and always 'worked and paid for' what he got.[27] He also worked as a police tracker and was proud of his bush skills.

He said of himself that he was half Irish and half a black man and that accounted for his cleverness. He embodied his mixed heritage, having Aboriginal facial features topped by wavy red hair. But Ethel remarked that he was 'particularly touchy about his colour' and did not like to be called a black fellow.[28] 'I reckon I'm as good as a white man', he declared.[29] It appears that in his late teens and early twenties he was accorded some degree of acceptance in white society, however for an 'uppity black' there was the ever-present danger of insult, abuse and rejection.

But what both changed his life and set him apart was his marriage at Gulgong in December 1898 to the sixteen-year-old white Ethel Page, who was five months pregnant. It was an extraordinary affront to rural society. Both Ethel and Jimmy suffered from rampant disapproval and outright ridicule. Ethel reported that she 'had to put up with a great many taunts'.[30] To escape the derision experienced in Gulgong, the young family went to work on a large farm in the district belonging to John and Sarah Mawbey.

Relations with the Mawbey family deteriorated largely, it seems, as a result of the ridicule heaped on Ethel by Sarah Mawbey and the local schoolteacher, Helen Katz, who boarded in the big farm-house. They told her that any white woman who married a black fellow was not fit to live. Once in their camp, Ethel later explained, 'I went down on my knees and prayed, "Oh Lord! Take me away from here. I cannot stand what these people are saying against me. Please let me go to some place where they'll let us alone, and we can be happy".'[31]

On 20 July 1900, Jimmy and his younger brother Joe called on the Mawbeys late at night, angered by their treatment of Ethel. He later explained what happened:

I went up the house and I said: 'Did you tell my missus that any white woman who married a black fellow ought to be shot? Did you ask my wife about our private business? Did you ask her what sort of nature did I have – black or white?' With that Mrs Mawbey and Miss Katz turned around and laughed at me with a sneering laugh . . . I struck Mrs Mawbey on the mouth with the nullah-nullah. Miss Katz said, 'Pooh, you black rubbish, you want shooting for marrying a white woman'. Then I got out of temper and got hammering them and lost control of myself.[32]

In addition to killing the two women, over the next week Jimmy and Joe killed three of the Mawbey children and four more people, including a one-year-old baby. After evading a massive man-hunt for four months the badly injured Jimmy was taken, tried and convicted of murder in November 1900. His execution was delayed until 18 January 1901 by the Executive Council of New South Wales so that it wouldn't cast a shadow on the celebrations marking the foundation of the new Commonwealth of Australia.[33]

During the second half of 1900 the colonial newspapers ran many stories about the Governor brothers and the long and arduous man-hunt that followed the murders at Mawbey's farm. They were the occasion for confirmation of popular prejudices about Aborigines in general and about half-castes in particular. There was broad consensus that half-castes were people torn between white and black heritages, between conflicting, warring bloods. They were inherently unstable and dangerous – always liable to atavism and to return the putative instincts of savage ancestors. No matter how assimilated Jimmy Governor appeared, how well he worked, how educated he was, the community was convinced that he nursed a hidden desire for revenge that burst forth uncontrollably during a week of mayhem.

As a result, folk wisdom about mixed-race marriage was confirmed and even more deeply entrenched. As the facts of the case emerged, the conclusion was that Jimmy's tragic mistake was not only to think he was as good as a white man but that he was so presumptuous that he developed a sexual relationship with a white girl, made her pregnant and then married her. Clearly rural society could not accept the union and would have never allowed the young couple any peace. Ethel's prayer to find somewhere where they would be left alone and be happy could never be answered – not in Australia and not in 1900. They had defied and challenged some of the deepest, most invincible taboos in colonial society. Jimmy's fateful journey to the gallows had the pitiless inevitability of a Greek tragedy. It was also a quintessentially Australian story. Jimmy was the Irish–Aboriginal boy who became a horse breaker and tracker, who combined the skills of hunter–gatherer and frontier bushman, and who saw himself as a bushranger in the tradition of Ned Kelly and Ben Hall.

Having examined the fate of the Governor brothers and the attitudes common at the time of Federation, it is time to consider the ways in which Australian society dealt with people of mixed descent.

CHAPTER 6

A Dying Race

The Australian colonists in the nineteenth century endlessly discussed the people they were dispossessing in their new land – in their newspapers, in meeting halls and churches, in private conversations and in public debates. Some spoke with personal knowledge of tribal people; others presumed they knew all they needed to know. But personal experience gained in the colonies was often not as important as the ideas that came from sources in Britain and America and filtered into Australia through innumerable channels. The Aborigines did have many humanitarian defenders – men and women who accepted the conventional Christian view that all people were of one blood, were all alike descendants of Adam and Eve and created in the image of God. But then there were others who emphasised the influence of the environment in shaping traditional society, and looked forward to rapid and effective assimilation.

However, for every public figure who defended the Aboriginal people there were more who condemned them and the balance shifted towards denigration as the nineteenth century progressed. Generalised pictures of savagery flourished in the colonial environment. The Port Phillip Protector of Aborigines, James Dredge, observed in 1845 that

> in almost every reference to the moral condition of the Aborigines of Australia which has obtained publicity, they are presented as a race of beings either entirely destitute of rational mind, and thus ranging only at the head of the order of inferior animals; or, if allowed to be men at all, are described as possessing such diminished mental capabilities, as exhibit such a humiliating specimen of the degradation of which human nature is susceptible, as to indicate their position at the very lowest point in the scale of rationality.[1]

Overseas controversies and debates echoed in colonial discourse with frequent local references to the 'great chain of being', to facial angles and cranial capacity, to phrenology and polygenesis, the laws of evolution, the survival of the fittest and dying races. In an anonymous report written in 1826 for the Methodist Missionary Society in London, the author explained that in New South Wales it was frequently argued that the Aborigines were a new production, forming a link 'in the grand chain between the human and brute creation', human in outward appearance but without mind, soul or intellectual powers.[2] At much the same time visiting French scientists reported that as a result of a careful examination of many Aboriginal heads they had confirmed their opinion as to the '*innate* deficiency of these poor people'.[3] The explorer Charles Sturt, an otherwise sympathetic observer of Aboriginal society, concluded that the whole appearance of indigenous heads 'would lead to the conclusion that they possess few of the intellectual faculties'.[4]

Phrenology was popular in the colonies in the middle of the nineteenth century, with practitioners performing in public halls in any town large enough to provide an audience. A Mr Knowles informed a Brisbane meeting in 1851 that he had examined many Aboriginal skulls and found that they were much thicker than those of Europeans. As a result, although black heads appeared to be the same size as white ones, they did not command an equivalent amount of 'thinking power'. Indeed, the smallness of the Aboriginal brain was responsible for 'all his miserable manifestations of mind'.[5] Given its apparent scientific method, phrenology appeared to be a plausible theory and means of explaining Aboriginal disadvantage. The Royal Navy captain J. L. Stokes was a sympathetic observer of their plight in colonial society but came to the conclusion that 'if the principles of that science are admitted to be true, these savages are woefully deficient in all the qualities which contribute to man's moral supremacy'.[6]

Phrenologists were called on to provide expert advice. A Mr Sohier gave evidence to the 1859 Victorian Legislative Council Select Committee on the Aborigines. He observed that judging from skulls in his possession any 'permanent improvement' would be a very difficult achievement. Their small brain and inferior temperament were great barriers to their ever being permanently improved.[7]

Darwin's theory of evolution was rapidly transmitted to the Australian colonies, stirring controversy, gaining adherents and influencing settler discussion about the Aborigines. The historian James Bonwick, who had written with great sympathy for the Tasmanian Aborigines, observed in 1888 that those who accepted 'the evolution doctrine as applied to the physical origins of man' regarded the Aborigines as being 'nearer than most existing peoples to the anthropoid apes'; they had many characteristics of 'transitional humanity'.[8] The prominent medical scientist W. Ramsay-Smith addressed the Adelaide Congress of the Australian Association for the Advancement of Science in 1907 on the subject of 'The Place of the Australian Aboriginal in Recent Anthropological Research'. He referred to the anatomical features that humans shared with the gorilla and chimpanzee. Of all the races studied, the Aborigines had 'furnished the largest number of ape-like characters'.[9]

It was scarcely surprising that colonists eagerly embraced the idea that the fate of the Aborigines was due to a struggle for existence over which human beings had little control. In a paper to the Advancement of Science Congress in 1890, James Barnard referred to the Tasmanian Aborigines and noted that it had 'become an axiom, that following the law of evolution and survival of the fittest, the inferior races of mankind must give place to the highest type of man'.[10] 'It seems a law of nature', the editor of *The Age* observed in 1888, that where two races at different stages of development were brought into contact 'the inferior race is doomed to wither and disappear'. The process, he believed, seemed to be in accordance with a natural law, which, while it might clash with human benevolence, was 'clearly beneficial to mankind at large by providing for the survival of the fittest'. In fact, human progress itself had been achieved by 'the spread of progressive races and the squeezing out of inferior ones'.[11] Archibald Meston, the Queensland ethnographer, adventurer and sometime politician, wrote a report for the colonial government about an exploring expedition he had led in the tropical rainforests. He considered the impending fate of the local Aborigines and referred to all such situations where

> the strong colonising race has treated harshly and contemptuously the weak race which it displaced. This is the history of all new countries, and the slaughter of the aboriginals by the invader is the one monotonously conspicuous fact in all the records of colonisation. No euphemism of expression or sentimentalism of thought can conceal that from the historian or the student of ethnology. In all human progress and the transition and rise and fall of nations we see the all-ruling influence of the law of the survival of the strongest . . .
>
> The Australian blacks are moving rapidly on into the eternal darkness in which all savage and inferior races are surely destined to disappear. All efforts to preserve them, though creditable to our humanity, is a poor compliment to our knowledge of those inexorable laws whose operations are as apparent as our own existence.[12]

A few years after he wrote this passage Meston became the Protector of Aborigines in southern Queensland. His belief that inexorable laws of evolution had condemned the Aborigines to extinction was probably shared by the great majority of his contemporaries. A successor of Meston, J. W. Bleakley, wrote an article in 1930 entitled 'Can Our Aborigines Be Preserved?' He remarked that the subject could hardly be said to be a keenly debated question for it seemed to be 'the generally accepted view that the extinction of the Australian Aborigines is inevitable'.[13]

Both Meston and Bleakley were deeply concerned about the racial mixture that had already taken place and the mixed-descent people who themselves were marrying – or at least cohabiting – and having children. Not surprisingly the Australian colonists had discussed what became known as the 'half-caste problem' in debates that witnessed the conjunction of imported ideas and local experience.

Sexual relations between European men and Aboriginal women began soon after first contact and continued during the early years of settlement, whether as a consequence of mutually agreed exchange, abduction and rape, or semi-permanent relationships. The absence of white women in all frontier areas and over long periods of time increased the incidence of interracial sex. This pattern first became apparent on the vast pastoral frontier in New South Wales and among the sealing gangs working along the coasts and among the offshore islands in southeastern Australia. An early missionary noted in his journal in July 1834 that there was 'scarcely a man within 40 miles of us Bond or Free who is not living in adultery, with these unhappy females'.[14] A colleague was equally distressed by the extent of sexual activity. Aboriginal women were, he thought, engaged in 'frequent and almost constant intercourse with voloptuous [sic] Europeans'.[15] A New South Wales Legislative Council Select Committee of 1845 solicited the views of prominent citizens all over the colony about the situation of the Aborigines. They were asked whether there was 'any disposition on the part of the white labouring population to amalgamate with the Aborigines so as to form families'. The overwhelming response was that while interracial sex was rampant, there was almost no inclination for white men to form permanent relations with their black lovers. A clergyman from the Western District of Victoria reported 'unhesitatingly' that promiscuous sexual commerce was carried out 'to an almost incredible amount'. At the far end of the colony, Brisbane's Reverend Gregor explained that 'abominable intercourse' was common and open 'to a disgusting extent'.[16]

The Committee's informants referred to several cases where white men had married half-caste women but there is surprisingly little discussion of resulting mixed-race children in the Australian colonies, and almost no relevant statistical information became available until the final decades of the nineteenth century. We have no real idea of how many half-castes there were. The absence of information may have indicated that they were few and far between. But it may have been the result of a fundamental lack of interest. Such children almost always grew up with their Aboriginal mothers and may not have been noticed. European interest and concern intensified later in the nineteenth and in the early twentieth centuries when mixed-race children of the second or third generation were observed and considered to be far too 'white' – too European – to be allowed to remain with their families.

But to observers with an ethnographic bent, the apparent absence of half-castes demanded an explanation and attracted the attention of scholars in far-off Europe and America. French scientists believed that one could 'scarcely quote any cross between Australians and Europeans'[17] and the influential Paul Broca denied the existence of half-castes altogether. He believed that everything tended to establish that the union of the white man and the Australian woman was but 'little prolific' and that any resulting children died at an early age. He was struck also by the absence of terminology in Australia for the products of racial mixing, believing that there was not 'a single word to designate the Mulattoes', yet in all countries 'where races of different colours mix, the language of the locality contains always distinct denominations for mulattoes of various shades. Nothing of the kind exists in Australia'.[18]

Many other scholars disputed the belief that there were no half-castes in Australia but the idea persisted into the twentieth century. In his Robert Boyle Lecture of 1919 Sir Arthur Keith declared that the

> British communities in Australia bred and exhibited the usual Saxon sense of race discrimination; almost from the first they drew a racial frontier between themselves and the native blacks, and so strictly has this frontier been maintained that there is no trace of the vanishing aboriginal blood in the veins of the new nationality.[19]

The question of Australian hybrids was a controversial one, attracting much attention in the scholarly literature during the middle years of the nineteenth century. Opponents of such scholars as Pouchet and Broca referred to the one isolated, distinctive community of mixed-blood Australians that was known overseas at the time – the one on the islands of Bass Strait and made up of Aboriginal women from Tasmania and the polyglot population of sealers. They had been described by Captain J. L. Stokes of

HMS *Beagle,* which was in Australian waters between 1839 and 1843. Stokes's account of his travels, the two-volume *Discoveries in Australia,* was published in 1846. He described the isolated lives of 'the Straitsmen', as they were known at the time. No longer dependent on the much-depleted seal colonies, they survived by fishing, hunting, gardening and collecting and selling the feathers of the migratory mutton-birds. Stokes was particularly interested in the young half-castes. There were twenty-five children, among whom were some 'fine looking boys'. They had a ruddy dark complexion with fine eyes and teeth.[20]

The Straitsmen and their healthy, competent children were taken as compelling evidence by ethnographers and biologists seeking to establish that races as different as the Europeans and Tasmanians could produce children who themselves could survive and breed. The prominent French anthropologist Paul Topinard explained in the early 1870s that in European scholarly circles until a few years previously only three or four instances were known of Aboriginal interbreeding with Europeans. Stokes had therefore provided an 'undoubted example' of the phenomenon.[21] In correspondence with the French consuls in Sydney and Melbourne, Topinard had been told that 'a great number of Australian mixed breed' were to be met with in the colonial towns and plantations. The German scholar Oscar Peschel also argued that Tasmanian women had given birth to numerous hybrids, although he thought that in many cases 'the natives themselves frequently destroy the half-castes'.[22]

This became a commonplace explanation in books written by the colonists and in the more theoretical works produced in

Europe and America that drew on local ethnographic observations. There did appear to be a problem that needed explaining: widespread and continuous sexual relations had produced very few children. One answer that became obvious only in the 1920s and '30s was the overwhelming impact of sexually transmitted disease, particularly gonorrhoea. Some nineteenth-century observers related the lack of children to the living conditions of Aborigines surviving precariously on the fringes of white society where women were, James Bonwick observed, 'subsisting upon the food of strangers and given up to drunkenness and indiscriminate licentiousness'. That to suppose such women capable of having offspring by either white or black would be 'to credit public prostitutes with fecundity'.[23] The South Australian missionary George Taplin pointed to the deleterious effects of heavy smoking and of excessive use of alcoholic drinks that injured and often entirely prevented fertility.[24]

For those who believed that Europeans and Aborigines were distinct species and therefore dysgenic, there was nothing to explain. The answer was obvious. But for those of a different view, the easiest explanation was that Aboriginal women either aborted their foetuses or killed the newborn half-caste children in one way or another, not that there was ever much direct evidence for this assumed widespread infanticide. Writing in 1845 of his experience in South Australia, explorer Edward Eyre asserted that infanticide was common in Aboriginal society and that half-castes appeared to be always destroyed.[25] In his *Recollections of Squatting in Victoria*, Edward Curr similarly argued that initially half-castes were destroyed at birth.[26]

Writing of Tasmanian half-castes, James Bonwick referred to 'these unhappy products of intercourse in the Bush' of 'the marriage of the hour', and that

> if permitted to see the light, seldom lived long in the tribe. The mother to conceal her shame, or repenting of her act, would often prevent the birth by abortion; or, if unsuccessful, would destroy the infant upon its entrance into the world. If the philoprogenitive instinct led her to spare her child, the husband or brother might avenge the family wrongs by a fatal blow.[27]

The Polish adventurer and explorer Paul de Strezelecki added further theories to the ongoing international debate, arguing that once an Aboriginal woman had had intercourse with a white man she was found 'to lose the power of conception with her own race'. He declared that hundreds of instances of this extraordinary fact were on record. It was a common occurrence in other parts of the world where tribal people were in contact with Europeans and followed a cogent but mysterious law of nature.[28] The questions at stake were serious enough to attract the attention of Charles Darwin who, in *The Descent of Man* of 1872, determined that Strezelecki's thesis had been disproved, as had the more general assertion that the 'native women of Australia and Tasmania' rarely produced children to European men. Darwin believed that this evidence had been shown to be 'almost valueless' because the half-castes were killed by the 'pure blacks'.[29]

The only detailed demographic study of a mixed-blood community before 1939 was carried out by the anthropologist N.B. Tindale on the Bass Strait Islands. Making use of the community's detailed genealogical knowledge, he reconstructed the growth of the resident population from the early nineteenth century. The first half-caste children were born between 1814 and 1822, and despite stories of the killing of the earliest offspring at birth, the evidence suggested that it was 'not very long before they were being permitted to live'. Indeed, it was clear that by 1830 children were welcome and by 1840 twenty were living.[30]

International interest in the half-caste question stimulated Australian ethnographers to gather relevant information in the last quarter of the nineteenth century. They were particularly concerned with Strezelecki's theory and provided abundant evidence of women who had borne both half-caste and full-blood children in different sequences. Writing of the Coranderrk station in Victoria, the superintendent John Green explained that he knew of many female half-castes who had had children to white men as well as to blacks. There were three women at Coranderrk who had each had children with their full-blood husbands.[31] George Taplin, the South Australian missionary, reported that he had known many women who had large families after bearing a half-caste child. Instances had occurred where the first child was fathered by a white man and yet a large family of black children followed. He knew of several mixed families where black children had both preceded and followed the birth of half-castes.[32]

In his survey of Victorian Aborigines published in 1876, R. Brough-Smyth commented that the colony's half-castes presented 'peculiarities that were of great interest'. The girls were generally a pale brown, usually called olive, he added. They did not show much red on their cheeks, while the boys had bright, clear complexions and some 'could not be distinguished from children of European parents'. There were ordinarily patches of light-brown hair mixed with the dark brown of their heads but he had never seen 'any peculiarity in the colour of the eye'. They partook in their 'form, features and colour' more of the character of their European fathers than their indigenous mothers. They had some facial characteristics that were obviously Aboriginal, but seldom was any one feature very strongly or coarsely marked. They were very like the people of southern Europe, while many would be passed by 'without remark in a crowd of English children'. Brough-Smyth remarked that what peculiarities the young half-castes might display when they reached maturity was not known. Some very quickly adopted European customs, while others preferred the society of the blacks. It seemed to depend on the manner in which they had been situated in their youth.[33]

Writing of his experience in South Australia, Taplin remarked that the pure blacks were not as healthy as the half-castes. It was always the case, he believed, that the children of two half-castes would be healthier and stronger than either the children of blacks or the children of a black and a half-caste. When two half-castes married, they generally had large and vigorous families. He could, he wrote, 'point to half a dozen such'.[34] The ethnographer John Matthew had much the same to say about half-castes in Queensland. Their greater vitality showed out with 'remarkable prominence'. He knew a woman called Jenny Lind who had been twice married, who had nine children and thirteen grandchildren, all of whom were living.[35] Such local evidence of the health and fertility of half-caste Australians appears to have had little impact on those many scholars who continued to insist upon the physical degeneracy of all people of mixed descent. This was evidence provided on the ground in Australia and had little impact on the grand theories.

One reason why there is little about half-castes in the extensive ethnographic literature of the time was that most interest was focused on the traditional Aborigines, who were considered to be unique relics of the Stone Age. It was widely believed that when it came to half-castes the blood stream had already been corrupted, the culture compromised. But equally the half-caste child did not appear to be a source of concern or anxiety in the 1870s and 1880s, although perceptive witnesses could already see a likely population explosion impending. Occasionally there were voices that presaged future policy and opinion. When giving evidence before a Victorian Select Committee on the Aborigines in 1858, Patrick Mitchell, a settler in the Port Fairy district, explained that he was concerned at the plight of the half-castes, and especially that of the girls. He appreciated that the Aborigines were particularly fond of their half-caste children and would not surrender them to the whites, but he urged that 'some means of attaining that end' should be implemented, thus 'averting the ruin to which these young girls are otherwise surely doomed'.[36] On the other side of the continent the Bishop of Perth wrote to the government in 1873 explaining his concern that

children and young persons of mixed blood, many of them more than half-European, are to be seen frequently throughout the Country, utterly neglected and abandoned to their fate; with no future before them but that of ignorance and vice, and depravity, of the most revolting character.[37]

It is possible to find other brief references to half-castes in the literature of the 1870s and 1880s, but it is rare that we can glean enough information to build up any sort of image about the individuals in question. In his book *The Last of the Tasmanians* James Bonwick wrote of Maryann, 'the half-caste' wife of Walter George Arthur. There was an etching in the book of the couple, well dressed and formally posed. She had, Bonwick wrote, the appearance of her mixed race. Her delicate hands, her dark eyes, her nose and mouth 'declared the native mother', while her broad and lofty forehead indicated the European descent of her father. There was

> not only vigour of intellect, but a strength of independence of will, stamped upon her expansive features. The base of her brain represented the portentous character of animal appetites, while the loftiness and breadth elsewhere exhibited the force of moral sentiments.

She was a woman who, placed in happier circumstances, could have been 'Czarina of Russia' and would have emulated the intellectual powers of a Catherine, though she might have betrayed 'an equal intensity of passions'.[38]

By the early twentieth century certain things had become clear in the settled districts of Australia. The Aboriginal communities were undergoing important changes. The full-blood population was declining year by year, and there were now reasonably reliable

statistics to prove it. Deaths outnumbered births every year, everywhere around the country. There seemed little reason to hope that
this inexorable long-term trend would be reversed, confirming
the almost universal belief that the Aborigines would die out in the
foreseeable future. In the late nineteenth and early twentieth centuries many districts buried the old king or queen, the last of the
local tribe. Old settlers could remember times when there were
very much larger indigenous populations. Local knowledge and
evolutionary theory conspired to place the idea of the dying race
beyond the reach of debate. The full bloods were a Stone Age
people who were living on borrowed time. They were temporal
anomalies.

There were still plenty of negative – or even positively hostile –
attitudes directed at the Aborigines at this time. This was certainly
the case in the frontier regions right across northern Australia, as
local turn-of-the-century newspapers attest. But among politicians
and officials in the state capitals, condescension was more apparent than condemnation. Sympathy tinged with guilt was a common
prescription. In the parliaments members spoke of the full bloods
as they would of an acquaintance with a mortal illness. There was
a sense of a debt owing, a need to do something to ease the passing, although it rarely found expression in significant financial
commitment even to basic welfare.

But half-castes were a different matter. It was becoming increasingly apparent that the mixed-blood population was not declining.
It was not going to disappear. In fact, the rate of increase seemed to
be speeding up, with widespread reports of large families of abundant and healthy children. Many of them were light-coloured and

looked like Europeans. In political and bureaucratic circles the belief began to grow that something must be done. Increasingly, the relevant discussion was couched in terms of threat and menace. Specific and obvious social problems associated with poverty, unemployment, poor housing and at best rudimentary education became tangled up with preconceived notions about the entrenched nature of mixed-blood people. Generations of scientific discussion filtered through and shaped popular perceptions. Half-castes did not fit into neat racial categories. They could not be placed easily in an evolutionary sequence. They presented White Australia with a social, a political and an intellectual problem.

Policy makers and legislators vacillated and fretted about what to do. Proposed policies of absorption ran up against the reality of rigid colour bars wherever the two communities lived side by side. The passionate commitment to White Australia and the concomitant belief that racial mixture was undesirable and dangerous made early-twentieth-century Australia a particularly troubling place for the mixed-blood, mestizo population. Governments and their officials became increasingly keen to pass legislation that restricted the freedom of Aborigines and half-castes more and more, rescinding the liberties considered normal by other Australians. But whatever was done, the population went on increasing, and so the half-caste problem continued to dog the dream of White Australia right up until the 1940s. And it was this problem that determined the shape of indigenous policy for two generations and caused grief and suffering to Aboriginal communities all over the country.

CHAPTER 7

A Problem

Emerges

In New South Wales it is possible to chart the growth and change of the indigenous population from 1882 when the Aboriginal Protection Board began to collect statistics each year and compare those figures with the official census that counted people of 'full descent' and others from 1891 onwards. In that State in 1882 there were 6540 people of full descent and 2379 of mixed parentage, with a total population of 8919. Over the next twenty years the total had fallen to 6915. But the most dramatic development was that the mixed or mestizo population had increased by 1500 to 3897, while the number of people of full descent had halved from 6540 to 3036. In 1897 people of mixed descent became the leading group for the first time. This had been pending for years. During the 1880s, deaths exceeded births every year among the full-descent group. The reverse was true of the mestizo. At some point in the late 1880s the increase of the group was larger than the decline of the full bloods. Protection Board figures for 1888 recorded a total increase of sixteen. It was a significant moment pointing towards demographic recovery in the Aboriginal and mixed-race population. However, apparently no one paid much attention to it at the time. There was certainly no mention of it in the outpouring of speeches, books and articles celebrating the centenary of European occupation of New South Wales. But the trend continued. The board recorded an increase of forty-four in 1889 and fifty-nine in the following year.[1]

The first report of the new Protector of Aborigines in 1882 carried a message of concern about the growing population of half-castes. The protector had already decided that they should not be permitted to 'grow into a pauper or quasi-gypsy class'. They should be taught and compelled to work for their own living and 'thereby ultimately merge into the general population'. Members of the Protection Board showed a keen interest in gaining power over Aboriginal and especially half-caste children to give them the authority to remove 'such children as they deem necessary' to mission schools and out of the control of their 'professed guardians', who continued to roam the country and live in camps.[2]

Members of the local parliament expressed similar views. Albert Gould, member for Patrick's Plains, observed that 'these poor people' who were the 'original owners of the soil' had given way before the advance of civilisation. In a few years' time 'there would not be a blackfellow in the country'.[3] This was the general view. However, some members spoke with concern about the young half-castes, the member for the Bogan, J. E. Kelly, warning his colleagues that there were upwards of 3000 young people under fourteen years of age. Many of them, he observed, 'knew no fear' and were indifferent as to whether they broke the law or not. In his opinion 'these

were an exceedingly dangerous element in the community' and
every possible care needed to be taken to make them good members of society.[4]

For its part the Protection Board continually sought to increase
its reach and authority and was finally enabled to do so as a result
of legislation in 1909, 1915 and 1918. The 1909 Aborigines
Protection Act defined an Aborigine as any full-blooded native
of Australia and any person apparently having 'an admixture of
aboriginal blood' who was in receipt of rations from the board. The
Amending Act of 1915 increased the power of the board to remove
children from their families. Prior to this, the board had to proceed
under the aegis of an earlier Apprentices Act that had general application and required the authorities to establish that a child targeted
for removal was neglected under the terms of further legislation.
The 1915 Act declared that the board could assume full control
and custody of the child of any Aborigine if after due enquiry
relevant officials were satisfied such action was in 'the interests of
the moral or physical welfare of such child'.[5]

By 1918 New South Wales had decided, as Victoria had done
thirty years earlier, to attempt to merge the mixed-blood population into the general community. Growing interest and concern
regarding the half-caste problem was apparent in the collection of
statistics relating to degrees of racial mixture. The 1920 report
of the Protection Board contained the following breakdown of
the State's 7000-strong indigenous population – Full-blood:
1238; Half-Caste: 4532; Quadroon: 1123; Octoroon: 335. The
board stated:

The elimination of these people of lighter cast presents in many instances a difficult problem seeing that they have been reared among Aboriginals all their lives, and all their connections and interests are with Aborigines. However, it is hoped that by a gradual process of elimination the problem will eventually be solved.[6]

In 1921 the board reported on the number of children 'rescued from camp life' and concluded that a continuation of the policy of 'disassociating the children from camp life must eventually solve the Aboriginal problem'.[7] As was so often the case with Aboriginal policy, various pressures were apparent. Saving money was one of them. But there was also deep unease about the growing – and potentially permanent – part-Aboriginal population. R. Scobie, a member of both parliament and the Protection Board from 1901 to 1918, warned his fellow legislators in 1915 of looming danger, for although there were only a few full bloods left, there were 6000 'of the mixed blood growing up'. It was, he declared, a danger to have 'people like that amongst us, looking upon our institutions with eyes different from ours'.[8]

The Victorian government led the way among the colonies with comprehensive legislation and then in 1886 dealt directly with the question of the half-caste population. During the 1840s the Port Phillip Protectorate was the most serious endeavour of the Colonial Office to provide for the protection and welfare of the local Aboriginal people. The new Victorian government established a parliamentary select committee in 1858 and two years later appointed an official seven-member board charged to 'watch over the Interests of the Aborigines'.[9] In 1869 legislation provided more extensive powers to the board, giving it authority to determine where Aborigines could live. During the 1870s there were six Aboriginal settlements that were home to about half the total population of 1000. The 1869 Protection Act provided a broad and inclusive definition of the term 'Aboriginal native' which included 'every aboriginal half-caste or child of a half-caste, such half-caste or child habitually associating and living with aborigines'.[10] The inclusive communities provided a sense of solidarity to their inmates, although the managers and missionaries continued to increase their control over almost every aspect of life and tried to determine the way the Aborigines dressed, kept their houses, raised their children and whom they married.[11]

During the 1860s and 1870s the 'majority of whites concerned with Aboriginal affairs' agreed on a policy of segregating as many Aborigines as possible – full blood and half-caste – on isolated reserves.[12] A Royal Commission of 1877 favoured the continuation of such inclusiveness, reporting that

> no distinction can be drawn between the blacks and the half-castes, for although a general impression appears to obtain that the half-caste is more easily educated and more readily civilized than the Aboriginal native, yet, the evidence given and our own observation lead to no such conclusion.[13]

There was a rapid change of mood among white administrators during the 1880s. At a meeting of station managers in 1882, representatives of the board recommended that measures be adopted to 'raise the half-castes to independence' and to merge them into the general population of the colony. The new policy was embodied in a draft bill prepared by the board and justified in a statement that explained the object aimed at was that 'the process of merging should be completed as soon as possible, after which all responsibility of the Government as regards [the half-castes] would cease – *finality* being thus attained'.[14]

The Aborigines Protection Law Amendment Act of 1886 determined that all half-castes under the age of thiry-four would have to leave the stations and not return without permission. They could receive support for a bridging period of three years but after that they had no claim whatever on the State. There has been considerable debate in the literature about the reasons for the sudden change of policy and the adoption of radically new measures. Several issues appear to have been relevant. Expulsion of the half-castes clearly saved money for a cash-strapped board preparing for the planned closure of some stations. It also broke the back of a vigorous protest movement centred during the 1870s and 1880s among the young educated half-castes living on Coranderrk station near Healesville. There was, in discussion among whites interested in Aboriginal matters, a strong sense that half-castes were owed nothing by society and that they would benefit morally by being forced to fend for themselves. A woman thought to be sympathetic to the full bloods wrote to the government in 1882, explaining that

[i]f the white or half-caste element were removed by hiring out, the question of management would be very much simplified. The present management has often been condemned, besides it is grossly unjust to foster a race of paupers at the expense of the State.

It is also unjust to pure Aboriginals that the bounty of the State – a just recompense for deprived rights and privileges – should be lavished on the offspring of white immorality. The principle therefore of eliminating the white element is not only a just one but the only one which the community will eventually tolerate.[15]

Beyond the more immediate, pragmatic concerns there was the matter of 'finality'. While enigmatic, and no doubt deliberately so, it is possible to determine what members of the board were referring to. It was clear to anyone who looked at the Victorian Aboriginal community that, as was the case everywhere else in Australia, the full-blood population was ageing, deaths outnumbered births by a considerable amount and the group in question would die out as both high scientific theory and popular wisdom had long predicted. On the other hand, the half-castes, forced away from the stations and their full-blood relatives and scattered through a much larger host population, would eventually be absorbed. In a statement issued to *The Age* in February 1888 the board explained:

It was intended to place all the half-castes out as opportunity offered: and it was expected that by the end of six years the majority would have obtained employment. The pure aboriginals, of which there are about 300, will be kept until the end of their days: but the opinion of the board is that in the course of a very few years the whole of them will have passed away.[16]

The manager of the mission station at Lake Condah in the Western District, the Reverend Stähle, returned to the sensitive subject in a report to the board in 1902, observing that as the blacks were 'dying out' and half-caste boys and girls were being sent to Industrial Schools, 'finality is greatly facilitated, and will, doubtless, be attained within a few years'.[17]

The Merging the Half-castes Act, as it became known, had a dramatic and, in many ways, a tragic impact on the Victorian Aboriginal community. Almost half of the estimated 600 station residents, as many as forty families and 160 children, were expelled from the missions and stations. The imposed legislative division between half-caste and full blood cut sharply through families, through social networks, friendships and generations. And the board enforced its regulations ruthlessly and meticulously, refusing to bow to many requests for a relaxation of the rules to allow extended families to remain together. Half-caste children remaining on the stations were removed at the age of fourteen and sent to Industrial Schools.

The board was also concerned with marriage and used its power to determine who could and could not live on the stations, seeking to prevent half-castes from marrying full bloods. In the annual report of 1888 it was explained that the policy of merging the half-caste population would be frustrated if the intermarriage of blacks and half-castes was encouraged.[18] In her study of the Framlingham Reserve near Warrnambool, Jan Critchett outlined the case of a full-blood Aborigine, Tokas Johnson, who wrote letters of complaint to both the Chief Secretary and the Victorian Governor because he was told that if he married a half-caste girl called Ina Lancaster he would have to leave his home. After waiting patiently for six years, Johnson secretly married another half-caste woman and when found out was initially told he would lose his rations. In the minutes of a board meeting it was recorded that the old man by 'his silly marriage with a half-caste woman had forfeited his claim for supplies'.[19]

All the evidence indicates that the families evicted from the Victorian stations after 1886 suffered severely from unemployment, poverty and malnutrition. The onset of the Depression in 1890 exacerbated an already dire situation. The belief that half-castes could become absorbed into the larger society paid scant attention to the hostility that they met when they sought employment, accommodation, healthcare or education. Furthermore, the late nineteenth and early twentieth centuries saw an intensification of racial consciousness and a desire for a White Australia. By 1910 the board was forced to reverse its policy of 1886 of drawing a sharp distinction between full blood and half-caste, and sought and achieved an amendment to the Act in order to assist destitute half-castes. In a letter to the Chief Secretary in June 1910 the board's change of mind was clearly declared. 'The half-caste', the minister was informed, 'is invariably the child of a black mother and is reared by her amongst the aborigines. Although not pure blacks, such half-castes are practically Aboriginals . . .'[20]

In South Australia it was estimated that in 1901 there were 800 half-castes out of a total of just over 5000 Aboriginal people, with a similar pattern of a slow increase due entirely to the growth of the mestizo population.[21] The local protector noted in 1911 that the half-castes and quadroons were steadily replacing the blacks, who were 'slowly but surely dying out'. Between 1901 and 1911 the full-blood population had declined by 622, while the half-caste component had increased by 188. The State's two most important Aboriginal communities – Point Pearce and Point Macleay – were home in 1910 to 344 half-castes and eighty-seven full bloods.[22] The protector's concern was that if the mixed-blood population were to be 'left in the camps' the State would soon have 'a race of nearly white people living like aborigines'.[23] The immediate solution he urged upon the government was to utilise the State Children's Act passed in 1895 that allowed the authorities to institutionalise destitute or neglected children. In that way children could be taught useful trades and occupations and be prevented from acquiring the 'habits and customs of the aborigines'. They would become useful, self-supporting members of the community, instead of developing into 'worse than useless dependants'.[24]

The protector's concerns were addressed by the State parliament in legislation of 1911 and 1923. The first Act was similar to legislation passed in Queensland and Western Australia between 1897 and 1905. The Chief Protector was given wide powers to control the lives of both Aborigines and half-castes; the second Act dealt more specifically with the provisions of training for half-caste children. While introducing the first of the two bills, Premier John Verran referred to the large half-caste population springing up who, because of 'their taint of colour', were excluded from the 'privileges of white people'.[25] But there was wide disagreement about the putative character of half-castes and what policies should be applied to them. 'Do what you like with them', J. G. Mosely insisted, 'they are black fellows, and will remain as such . . .' They also had 'all the bad instincts of the whites'.[26] But A. H. Peake thought otherwise. They were as much civilised as the parliamentary members themselves. Indeed, they were 'Aborigines only in name'; black in name but not in nature.[27]

The Aborigines (Half-Caste Children) Bill was introduced into the South Australian Parliament in 1921 but failed to pass through all stages. Minister William Hague explained that by giving the State Children's Department power over half-caste children the government was making another attempt to solve the 'ever-growing problem of the half-caste'.[28] At Point Pearce there were ninety children between one and thirteen years and eighty-one at Point Macleay. The problem was getting more difficult every year, Hague declared. By taking the children away and raising them in State institutions they could be absorbed into the community. While they remained on the stations they would 'always be half-caste children'.[29] Members who supported the legislation did so for predictable reasons. James McLachlan believed the half-castes must be controlled because nine times out of ten they seemed to acquire 'all the vices of their parents but none of their virtues'.[30] Peter Reedy was willing to go further than the bill allowed, arguing that if the State was going to take the children away 'then you must remove them from their environment, so that they will forget all about where they belong and the customs of their people'.[31] J. B. Randell thought that while the problem of dealing with the Aborigines was not difficult,

> the task of making the half-caste a satisfactory citizen is more difficult. To expect to do it in one generation is to attempt the

impossible. They are half wild, and the other half contains the worst elements of our civilization.[32]

But the surprising feature of the debate was the strong opposition to taking children away from their families and communities. Peter Allen pointed to the prejudice that half-castes would experience in the wider community and that they were far better where they were. Unless it could be established that children were neglected, the State had no right to take them away.[33] Malcolm McIntosh asked the minister some very pointed questions. 'If the taint of blood' was the only fault, he remarked,

> why should the child be taken from the mother and placed in a probably worse environment? I think the people who had this country before the white man are entitled to special consideration and privileges. I do not think the Minister should ask power to take children away from their mothers because they are half-castes . . .[34]

The opposition was strong enough to cause the suspension of the bill, which was brought back to parliament two years later. While introducing the Aborigines (Training of Children) Bill of 1923, William Hague explained that Aboriginal women who had children by European men generally returned to the local communities where they grew up, helping to form a 'varied agglomeration of half-castes, quadroons and octoroons' that constituted a very difficult problem for mission staff to deal with. The intention was to send fifteen-year-old children to State orphanages and training

institutions.[35] But the bill again faced concerted opposition –
probably the most determined resistance to the removal of children
in any Australian parliament during the first forty years of the
twentieth century. Thomas McCallum declared that Aborigines
had the same love for their children 'as have the best of the white
population'. He told his colleagues:

> I am absolutely opposed to anything that will interfere with the
> family life of these people. I will not see children torn from their
> parents unless those children are absolutely neglected and are
> going to perdition. If they are living their lives according to their
> own way I am not going to assist in breaking their hearts by taking
> their children away.[36]

South Australia conducted a Royal Commission into Aboriginal
policy in 1913. It provides the reader with a useful compendium of
attitudes among officials, missionaries and activists in 'settled'
Australia in the period between Federation and World War I. Much
attention was given to the question of half-caste children. A key
recommendation of the report was that it was desirable to separate
'as much as possible the full-bloods from the half-caste natives',[37]
each living in discrete communities. The Chief Protector,
W. G. South, spoke approvingly of the half-caste who, he said, was
a 'better man than the blackfellow'. He thought it would be a disgrace if that were not the case. Looking forward to the time when
all would be nearly white, he observed that if they were to remain
'a race of aboriginals' he would not trouble more about them 'than
merely feeding them'. But the mestizoes were members of another
race, and it was increasing in numbers.

South told the commissioners that he made use of the Children's Act to take away children that he found in the bush and whom he thought were not receiving proper care and control. But his task of getting control of the children was not always an easy one, as he explained in evidence:

> I have found a difficulty in getting possession of the children in the interior. In some cases the magistrates have refused to commit them to the care of the State Children's Department. In other cases they have said that the Act does not apply . . . I think, too, that the police as a rule do not care to be taking the children away from their parents. They sympathise with the mothers. I myself sympathise with the mothers; but I think that the child is a more important consideration than the mother. The mother is usually a black woman living in comparative savagery and the child is the offspring of a white man, and I think it is a pity that that child should be brought up amongst the natives . . . Some people say that they will go back to the black's camp, but I say that they never do that, because they will not know a black's camp. If you take a child, practically white, from the centre of Australia and bring it down here and train it, it will not go back, because it will not know anything about it.[38]

Protector South was supported in his policy of removing half-caste children by a number of witnesses, none more prestigious than E. C. Sterling, Professor of Physiology at Adelaide University. In his opinion the more children who could be taken away from their parents the better. He thought they should be removed at an early age – at about two or three – after they had been weaned but while they still had 'the attractiveness of infancy'. When they were 'caught young' they were far less inclined to go back to the ways of the natives. The professor was asked whether he thought the children's experience of two years with their mothers might 'seriously interfere' with them. He replied:

> No. There would not be time for them to establish habits and customs. I am quite aware that you are depriving the mothers of their children and the mothers are very fond of their children; but I think it must be the rising generation who have to be considered. They are the people who are going to live on.[39]

CHAPTER 8 | # Outcasts in the Outback

In 1901, Queensland, Western Australia and South Australia, along with its dependent Northern Territory, shared many of the characteristics of the other states in regard to its treatment of the indigenous population. In the southwest of Western Australia, southern Queensland and the closely settled parts of South Australia, European occupation was two, three or even more generations old. Dispossession of the Aborigines had been completed many years before. Diminished, remnant and often impoverished communities lived in fringe camps and on pastoral stations or performed casual itinerant labour on farms and selections. They also hunted, foraged and fished when they were able, maintaining a precarious independence half in and half out of white society.

But each state also had a vast tropical hinterland, home to thousands of Aborigines with little or no experience of Europeans, living undisturbed in ancient homelands. Frontier conflict continued in many districts. While there were fewer half-castes than in the southern districts their presence was, if anything, more troubling to the white pioneers. This was so for a number of reasons. In the whole of northern Australia, only the coastal strip of Queensland and its immediate auriferous hinterland supported a substantial white population. In western Queensland, the Top End and the Kimberley there were only a few thousand white men, very few white women and there seemed little realistic prospect of an imminent demographic boom. A few hundred half-castes scattered across the Darling Downs or Western Australia's Great Southern region might be seen as creating social problems, or as a public nuisance, but they didn't threaten to swamp the resident white population.

Added to this straightforward but highly significant numerical question was the ever-present nagging concern about whether white men, let alone white women, would ever be able to settle permanently north of latitude 20°S. There was never any doubt in anyone's mind that half-castes were thoroughly and comfortably at home in the tropics. To make matters worse, there were thriving communities of Asian and Melanesian men and the local Aborigines displayed a disturbing tendency to prefer to work, fraternise and sleep with them rather than with Europeans. The visible and worrying appearance of part-Asian and part-Melanesian children in the Aboriginal camps seemed likely to undermine White Australia's tenuous and contested hold on the whole of the tropical north.

One of the best-known pioneers of and spokesman for tropical Australia was Robert Logan Jack. In his 1922 book *Northmost Australia* he wrote:

This northern land is thinly peopled by a feeble folk inevitably doomed to vanish from the face of the earth within the current century. Fair dealing, kindness, philanthropy and Christianity alike have proved their inability to stay the operation of a natural law, mysterious and deplorable though the law may be.

Logically, it may be assumed as a corollary that the more the native blood is diluted the better. To any studmaster or student of eugenics the idea of leaving the future of the north to a breed tainted at its fountainhead is in the last degree repugnant, and politically is full of danger.[1]

The Aboriginal population presented many problems to the politicians and administrators in Perth, Adelaide and Brisbane, even if their personal experience of frontier conditions was often minimal. But at the turn of the century there was a growing consensus that 'something must be done'. Of the many complicated questions that seemed to demand an answer, the half-caste problem was foremost in view. It was a difficulty that clearly had a future and not merely a past. It was harder to ignore these people and, more especially, children who were part-European; the product, it was ruefully admitted, of white men's weakness and lack of self-control.

Each of the three colonial/state parliaments passed legislation around the turn of the century to deal with their Aboriginal population. Queensland led the way in 1897 and provided an admired model that was followed by Western Australia in 1905 and South Australia in 1911, just before the federal takeover of the Northern Territory.

Queensland's The Aboriginals Protection and Restriction of the Sale of Opium Act came into force in January 1898.[2] It provided the structure for the management of Aboriginal affairs until the 1960s. Sweeping powers were conferred on the government and its officials by section nine that declared the Minister could 'cause every Aboriginal within any District' to be removed to, and kept within the limits of, any reserve. Authority was also conferred to make regulations providing for the care, custody and education of Aboriginal children and for the transfer of any deserted or orphaned half-caste child to an orphanage. The legislation defined a half-caste as any person being the offspring of an Aboriginal mother and 'other than an aboriginal father'.

The two protectors appointed under the legislation – Archibald Meston and Walter Roth – showed early concern for half-caste children who, it appeared, were more likely than their full-blood contemporaries to be found living with Europeans, often in appalling conditions. The general settler view was that it was legitimate to take mixed-blood children away from parents and kin because they were half-European and needed to be 'saved' from their Aboriginal relations. The argument was that any experience with white people represented an improvement, a step upward on the ladder of civilisation.

The reality was often very different, as Roth found when investigating the circumstances of a series of children who came to his notice. There was Tommy, a 16-year-old girl who had been travelling as a boy with a white stockman for eight years.[3] Jack Baker at twelve or thirteen was sent to Yarrabah. He had been travelling with a circus company for 'some seven years'. The manager handed him over to the protector because he was 'getting beyond control'.[4] Dolly, a half-caste girl of thirteen, had been in Normanton with a Mrs M 'in whose employ she had been for ten years past'. Mrs M sought the local protector's permission to send the girl to a nearby station. Roth refused and the girl was handed over to the police, who discovered she was seven months pregnant. In his annual report to parliament Roth wrote:

> The girl having been with her mistress so many years without receiving any wages, and only possessing the two articles of clothing which she stood up in, the Protector asked Mrs M what she was prepared to do for her, but could get no satisfaction.[5]

There was Flora, a half-caste of about eight years who had become 'unmanageable'. She had been given to Mr W about twelve months previously by a local station owner.[6] Another young girl referred to as N had been working and living with Europeans to whom she had been given by the police. She had run away but was caught and taken back to her 'owners'. Roth was convinced that she had been cruelly treated,

> sworn at, beaten and kicked; she showed me a scar which she ascribed to her late employer's boot; she apparently had no blanket, and certainly received no wages – the poor thing had proved a hard-working willing slave. I considered her about fifteen years old, if that, notwithstanding that she had had a baby (now dead) a good twelve months before.[7]

Even when white families were more considerate the outcome was often disastrous. Roth observed that the time arrived sooner or later when the half-caste girl realised she was a pariah among the very people, probably ever since she could remember, that she had associated with as an equal. She had been taught to 'regard the full-blood with contempt, and the half-caste male as her inferior' and yet knew that she would never be acceptable as the wife of a white man. 'The end of these half-caste girls', Roth confided, 'is prostitution'.[8]

Although many children taken from their European 'owners' were sent away to government reserves or mission stations, it was more common in Queensland to send whole families away and certainly mothers and dependent children. When Archibald Meston was asked by members of the 1913 South Australian Royal Commission whether he thought half-caste children should be taken from their parents, he replied: 'No. They are fond of their parents. I do not think the companionship of the mother would be detrimental to the child.'[9]

While it was true that Queensland typically removed whole families to isolated reserves and missions, the children were frequently dispatched to dormitories once they had arrived at their destinations. Another characteristic of Queensland policy was to enforce the most rigid segregation between the reserves and the general community. Walter Roth was opposed to even allowing inmates to leave the reserves to participate in sporting contests. In his annual report for 1905 he explained and justified his policy. He sought to provide Aborigines with every legal protection when they were living in contact with Europeans, while 'making the isolation complete when once removed from it'. He took the opportunity of presenting to the parliament the general principles that guided him, explaining that the isolation of, and restricted intercourse between the weaker race and the stronger, so long as the preservation of the former continues to be the goal to which, as humanitarians, we are striving – is one that was accepted by the late Herbert Spencer after long study of ethical and historical problems. 'It seems to me', said the philosopher, 'that the only forms of intercourse which you may with advantage permit, are those which are indispensable for the exchange of commodities . . . No further privileges should be allowed to people of other races, and especially to people of the more powerful races, than is absolutely needful for the achievement of these ends'.[10]

But while Roth congratulated himself on the integration and intermarriage of half-castes dispatched to the missions, he was rigidly opposed to marriages with non-Aborigines. And this continued to characterise Queensland policy during the first decades of the twentieth century, the annual report of the Aborigines Department declaring in 1923 that the marriage of full-blood women to whites or aliens was rigidly tabooed. Half-castes were encouraged to 'mate with their own kind' or 'to marry back' with full bloods. The objective in mind was clearly declared. In order to combat 'the half-caste' evil, it was essential that the gulf between white and black should be widened as far as possible. This was the only way to protect the Aborigines from 'hopeless contamination', as well as 'safeguarding the purity of our own blood'.[11] The Departmental Report for 1919 estimated that half of the State's Aborigines were half-castes, which indicated that they had already suffered 'a 25 percent infusion of white blood' and it was indisputable that the European population had also been 'contaminated to an extent to warrant serious reflection'.[12]

In 1921 the Home Secretary William MacCormack was even blunter when addressing parliament in a debate about providing funds for Aboriginal settlements. The half-caste, he observed, was a most unfortunate individual and it should be their policy not to give opportunities 'for getting any of these half-castes in Queensland'. He had, he said, made that the policy of the department,

> and had found it a very good policy. The girls could marry men of their own race, live in the settlements, rear families there, and not have half-castes having all the aspirations and ideas of white people, but who had to put up with the position assigned to the half-caste.[13]

In 1929 the department reported a further increase of the half-caste population and confessed that the 'cross breed element' provided the most difficult part of the problem to deal with. The individuals in question seldom made either 'a steady white or a contented black'. The superior intelligence inherited from their white progenitors was 'generally nullified by the retarding instincts of the blacks'. The current policy was to check as far as possible 'the breeding of half-castes, by firmly discouraging miscegenation'. Every effort was made to encourage the marriage of people under control with their own race.[14]

Concern about half-castes in Queensland intensified in the early 1930s. The responsible minister, Home Secretary E. M. Hanlon, told his parliamentary colleagues in 1932 that the 'half-caste problem' was the outstanding difficulty of his department. Backbench members agreed. J. C. Peterson, the member for Mackay, remarked that any action the minister took to retard the increase in the number of half-castes would meet with the approval of all concerned. J. A. C. Kenny, member for the far northern electorate of Cook, concurred. The government, he argued, would have to tackle the problem sooner or later. 'In my opinion', he declared,

> the best thing that could happen would be for the department to encourage the half-castes to marry into the black race. The intermingling of the half-castes with the worst type of the white race can only produce a mongrel race in this state.[15]

The Reports of the Aborigines Department for 1932 and 1933 anxiously recorded annual increases in the half-caste population. It had become a matter that was causing grave concern in all states. Looking back on past endeavours to check 'this evil', the report recalled how officials had sternly attempted to prevent miscegenation. The marriage of whites and Aborigines, 'unfortunately not discouraged in earlier years', had been absolutely prohibited and every encouragement had been given for 'these women to marry amongst their own race'. Regulations had been framed to ensure strict control of women working in the community who were removed to the settlements if 'found to be promiscuous'. In calling for greater powers the department estimated that no more than 30 per cent of mixed-blood people were of European extraction, 'the others being of Asiatic or Polynesian breed'. This latter element, the report for 1932 asserted, already presented a serious social evil because they did not come under the aegis of existing legislation.[16]

At the department's behest the parliament passed in 1934 an

amendment to the original 1897 legislation, greatly extending the capacity to control the lives of the mixed-blood community. A new, much more inclusive definition of a half-caste was provided. It now embraced anyone with an Aboriginal grandparent or with two mixed-blood grandparents. It included any person of Aboriginal or Pacific Island extraction who lived with or associated with Aborigines. But the net was cast even wider to gain control of anyone who, in the opinion of the Chief Protector, was 'in need of the control and protection of this Act'.[17]

In his second reading speech to parliament Hanlon was quite frank about the purpose of the legislation, explaining that it was aimed particularly at taking control of all Asiatic and Island people who were 'crossed with Aborigines'. It was a measure that would allow the government to protect the targeted individuals 'not only from white people but also from themselves'.[18]

Queensland Aboriginal policy was subjected to numerous new pressures during the second half of the 1930s. Plans were drafted to establish separate, distinct, half-caste communities but the necessary money was not forthcoming. Policies pursued in Western Australia and the Northern Territory to encourage the marriage of half-caste women to white men were viewed with disquiet and Queensland authorities stressed the continuing influence of Asian and Pacific Island ancestry. The Chief Protector reminded the members of parliament that while such proposals might be suitable in some special cases of 'quadroon and lighter types with definite European characteristics', not every half-caste was the product of European breeding. Indeed, quite a large proportion were of 'alien blood more akin to the aboriginal race itself, such as

Pacific Island, African, Malay and others of Asiatic origin'.[19] A year later the department's annual report observed that the views of most of the authorities in Queensland 'disputed the wisdom of measures to encourage the absorption of these breeds'.[20]

When new legislation was debated in the parliament in 1939 the members showed little indication of having adopted a more tolerant attitude towards half-castes. W. L. Dart, the member for Wynnum, declared that the half-caste was 'a danger to the population'. In fact, Dart was of the opinion that he should be 'restricted in such a way as to prevent any further mixing with the whites' because 'we want to keep our race white'. What was more, 'we do not desire to see any more half-blooded people born into this world'.[21] Other members suggested the complete segregation of half-caste from black, and the taking of half-caste children to be reared as whites. H. M. Russell, the member for Hamilton, declared:

> The greatest evil of all, I think, has been the curse of the breeding of half-castes. We know very well that a great number of them are the offspring of aboriginals and fairly low-type settlers, whether white or yellow, and that these coloured people, the half-castes and quarter-castes, are looked upon as the pariahs of society. They have no social standing, and are shunned alike by the black man and the white man. That has been so in every country of the world where there is mixed population. Even in India the Eurasians are not treated with any respect, either by the white population or by the Hindus themselves. The half-castes in Queensland are a legacy that has been left to us, and we are endeavouring to eradicate or modify it.

It has been suggested that there should be intermarriage between half-castes and white people, so that eventually the half-caste blood will be absorbed or will be overwhelmed by the blood of the white race. That might be a long process. It seems to me if that course was adopted eventually the half-caste population would disappear. In the meantime, what we have to prevent if we possibly can is the increase of the half-caste population. The full-bloods are going out of existence. They are doomed, no matter what we do, but the half-caste population exists in very large numbers.[22]

The South Australian government and its officials living in Alice Springs and Darwin began to express concern about the growing number of half-castes from the 1890s onwards. The surgeon and Protector of Aborigines, Dr F. Goldsmith, reported in 1899 that half-caste numbers were increasing and that there were over fifty of all ages he knew of between Darwin and Katherine.[23] His successor, W. G. Stretton, estimated that in 1909 there were 150 half-castes in the whole Territory.[24] The usual prejudices were frequently voiced. The senior South Australian official Cecil Strangman was convinced half-castes inherited 'the vices of both races'.[25] Chief Justice C. J. Dashwood observed that among his contemporaries some held that both men and women were 'worse in disposition in every way'.[26] The notorious central Australian policeman, W. H. Willshire, considered them 'a very undesirable breed, with the white man's intelligence and the aborigine's cunning and treachery all combined'.[27]

In his annual report for 1899 Dashwood warned the government that the question 'as to what shall be done with the half-caste children will shortly need to be raised'.[28] Encouraged by the South Australian premier, C. C. Kingston, Dashwood prepared legislation modelled on the Queensland Act of 1897 entitled 'An Act for the Protection and Care of the Aboriginal and Half-Caste Inhabitants of the Province of South Australia'. A half-caste was defined as any person being an offspring of an Aboriginal mother and other than an Aboriginal father. Like its Queensland model, the legislation provided nominal protection against the worst abuses and most blatant discrimination while at the same time exercising unprecedented controls over Aboriginal society. But the bill, having passed the lower house in Adelaide, was defeated in the Legislative Council by conservatives strongly opposed to the premier.

The desire to control half-caste children ran strongly through the comments and correspondence of many of those who had an interest in the Aborigines, whether official or personal. The Alice Springs Protector, J. Mackay, proposed that half-caste girls 'not older than seven years of age' should be taken from their families and sent to training institutions in Adelaide.[29] The explorer Ernest Giles advocated segregated schooling and the collection of half-caste children in a boarding school in Darwin. Their numbers were rapidly increasing and he feared they would become 'an uneducated menace to Society'.[30] Dashwood had similar plans in mind, urging the government to remove mixed-blood children from Aboriginal camps and to place them in a boarding school where they could be kept away from 'their old associations' and trained to become useful servants.[31]

The same scheme was proposed by Dr Herbert Basedow, who briefly held the position of Chief Protector of Aborigines in 1911. He believed that one of the first steps to be taken was to gather all the half-caste children living with Aborigines. The police, he thought, could do the job and while the mothers would object, the future of the children would 'outweigh all other considerations'. Basedow's successor, the eminent scientist Baldwin Spencer, entirely agreed with the proposal to remove all the children from the camps. There was, he believed, much to be said in favour of the establishment of an institution for half-castes. But its existence would, he thought, have at least one serious drawback. It would indicate governmental recognition of mixed marriages, and more especially of 'irregular intercourse between the black and white races', which should be 'discountenanced as much as possible'. A single institution housing half-castes would be an acute embarrassment. Better, Spencer declared, to distribute them 'amongst the different mission stations'.[32]

When the South Australian politicians came to debate legislation for the Aborigines in the Northern Territory they were aware of the thousands of traditional people still beyond the control of government. They were also concerned about the growing numbers of half-caste children. Thomas Burgoyne declared that it was both preposterous and cruel to allow them to 'herd with full-blooded blacks'. They should be taken from the camps and brought up as 'children of the State'. He had heard, he said, 'a deal about the barbarity of taking the child from its mother' and the distress it caused. That was all very well when applied to Europeans, 'but it did not apply in the same degree, if at all, to aborigines'.[33]

CHAPTER 9 | 'Very Immoral

Subjects'

As in Queensland and the Northern Territory, concern about half-castes intensified in Western Australia during the 1890s. Up until that time the small number of mixed-descent individuals had not experienced significant legal discrimination. In the 1891 census they were counted with the white population and in 1893 those who possessed the required qualification were given the right to vote. In his study *Not Slaves, Not Citizens: The Aboriginal Problem in Western Australia 1898–1954*,[1] Peter Biskup noted that the part-Aboriginal population practically doubled between 1891 and 1901. White attitudes were also shifting dramatically. 'Suddenly, almost overnight', Biskup believed, 'the government and the country came to realize that they had an additional problem on their hands'.[2]

In 1896 the Aborigines Protection Board received a report written by George Marsden about the colony's north, where 'many half-caste children were beginning to appear'. In almost every case they were being brought up by their Aboriginal mothers, the putative father in most cases 'disclaiming the child altogether'. Marsden posed the question of what was to be the future of the children but knew in advance how they would turn out. It was certain, he wrote, that they would have all the bad points of the black 'with none of the good points of the white man'. The answer to what should be done was clear. They should be taken away at five and sent to institutions. The absent father, if known, should be given a say in the matter but not the mother, because she would 'in most cases naturally prefer the child to remain with her'. Her view should be overruled for the child's sake. Marsden spoke widely with northern white residents about the problem and he found that many agreed with his views. 'I have', he wrote,

> spoken to the Warden of the Kimberley Goldfields, also to . . . the Resident Magistrate at Derby and several of the older settlers and they are all of the opinion that it is extremely desirable that such half-castes should be taken away from their country and properly brought up not only because they are partially 'white blooded' but that growing up with the blacks and having some of the intelligence of the whites, they will become extremely dangerous.[3]

Henry Prinsep, the Secretary to the Aborigines Protection Board, was a strong and persistent advocate of taking half-caste children away. In justifying his ambitions in his annual report of 1906 he explained that most were usually found in communities where the influence was towards laziness and vice and that it was 'our duty' not to allow children whose blood was half-British to grow up as vagrants and outcasts.[4] In his next annual report Prinsep again warned that if the swelling band of half-caste children grew up wandering with their Aboriginal families, they would eventually be 'not only a disgrace but a menace to our civilization'.[5]

Prinsep outlined his frustration, reminding the political leaders that the law then in existence did not empower him to 'take possession of them, or interfere with them'.[6] He was required to obtain the consent of parents before children could be institutionalised 'for their benefit and education'. Without any special legal authority a certain amount could be done by persuasion but 'the natural affection of the native mothers' had much stood in his way.[7]

An additional problem confronting increasingly anxious West Australians was that in the north Asian men were fathering half-caste children and even marrying their Aboriginal mothers. A policeman based at La Grange Bay south of Broome wrote in 1901 to G. S. Olivey, the Travelling Inspector of Aborigines, highly critical of the law for allowing such marriages. Such permissiveness, he declared, was 'the most absurd action ever permitted'. Resulting children, he predicted darkly, would have 'all the vice of the Asiatic' mixed with the black blood of the mother. They would assuredly prove a menace 'if not criminals to the country'.[8] Olivey himself didn't need any encouragement from the concerned policeman. Writing of conditions in Broome, he noted that although Aboriginal women married to Asians and West Indians were very happy and contented and had 'certainly been raised above their ordinary level', the practice of allowing such unions should be stopped by law.[9] The apparent success of Broome's interracial marriages was in fact the problem, Henry Prinsep declaring that the intermixing of natives with Asiatics, which is rapidly increasing, is, in my opinion, bad for the future of the race. Although Mr Olivey's and other reports show that the Asiatics, as a rule who possess themselves of native wives treat them very kindly, this very kindness will probably fill some of the Northern districts with a mongrel race, very inimical to future quietude.[10]

A year later Prinsep was still urging the government to give him greater powers to control the State's half-caste children. In fact, 'the conditions and proper government of half-castes' was one of the principal questions that had been exercising his mind. There was a sense of urgency. The children were growing up and would soon arrive at an age when they could either be a benefit or a menace to the State, and the prognosis was that without significant changes in the law and its administration, they would become a menace. Prinsep believed it was his government's duty to 'make good citizens of them by every means in our power'. He again reminded his superiors that he had on a number of occasions urged the introduction of legislation that would make him 'the official guardian of all these children'. If the power was granted to him he would be able in a very short time to have all of them placed under proper care. And it was a matter that demanded immediate action. Explaining his frustration, Prinsep observed that during his years in the Aborigines Department he had seen numerous half-caste children growing from children to adults. In the process, he confided, they had 'slipped out of my hands'.[11]

Prinsep got his way, and amending legislation was introduced into parliament in 1904. Clause 36 gave the protector power to place any child of a half-caste or Aboriginal mother in an industrial home. While introducing the bill the Minister for Lands, J. M. Drew, explained that as the law stood there was no power to take such action. Consequently the half-castes, 'who possess few of the virtues and nearly all the vices of whites', grew up to be mischievous and 'very immoral subjects'. Confiding in his fellow members, the minister said that while it might appear to be a cruel thing 'to tear away an aboriginal child from its mother' it was necessary in some cases to be cruel to be kind.[12]

The powers conferred on the West Australian Aborigines Department were impressive. As Biskup pointed out, any Aborigine who was not in 'useful employment' could be removed to a reserve or expelled from any town or municipality that had been declared a 'prohibited area'. The Chief Protector became the legal guardian of Aboriginal children and had been accorded the right to exercise the general care, protection and management of property, including the right to take possession of, retain, sell or dispose of any such property. A part-Aboriginal woman could not marry a non-Aborigine without official permission, and if she cohabited with a non-Aborigine the man in question was liable to prosecution.[13]

The widely perceived need for such restrictive legislation was confirmed by Queensland's Chief Protector of Aborigines, Walter Roth, who conducted a Royal Commission into the Condition of the Natives, reporting to the West Australian government at the end of 1904. Writing of the 500 or so half-caste children enumerated in a recent census, Roth declared that if they were left to their own devices under the existing state of the law, their future would be one of vagabondism and harlotry. Police officers and resident

magistrates had given Roth almost unanimous advice. Carnar-
von's magistrate predicted the children in his town would spend
most of their lives in gaol or as prostitutes if something was not
done with them. They should be sent to a reformatory or a mission,
whether their parents wished it or not. His colleague in Broome
thought the children should be taken right away because so long as
they remained in their own district it was impossible to do anything for them. Derby's magistrate considered that it was the young
half-castes 'that should be got at'. They grew up to lives of prostitution and idleness, he advised, and if they could be taken away from
their surroundings much good might be done with them.[14]

Soon after the passage of the 1905 legislation the Aborigines
Department began to remove young half-castes from their camps
and communities right across the northwest. The Chief Protector
reported to parliament in 1907 that instructions had been given to
protectors and police to 'try and collect these children' and send
them to the Catholic mission at Beagle Bay, although 'some little
difficulty' was experienced in getting the parents to part with them.
One of the local officials involved, Travelling Inspector James
Isdell, responded by remarking that he was glad to receive tele-
graphic instructions at Hall's Creek to arrange the transport of all
half-castes to the mission. He estimated there were approximately
eighty children in the northwest who should be targeted, particularly because of what he considered the open indecency and
immorality of the camps. Youngsters were able to hear 'vile conversations ordinarily carried on' that they were liable to repeat. Isdell
confided in his superior that in collecting and transporting the
children 'the question of separating them from their mothers

against their will' was sure to crop up. But the overriding concern was the 'future welfare of the youngsters'. In justification he wrote:

> I am convinced from my own experience and knowledge that the short lived grief of the parents is of little consequence compared with the future of the children. The half-caste is intellectually above the aborigine, and it is the duty of the State that they be given a chance to lead a better life than their mothers. I would not hesitate for one moment to separate any half-caste from its aboriginal mother, no matter how frantic her momentary grief might be at the time. They soon forget their offspring.[15]

During October 1909, Isdell set out to collect all the half-castes living around Fitzroy Crossing. He spent thirty-three days, often in extreme heat, carrying out his mission. When he had finished he reported that he had 'pretty well cleaned' the Fitzroy District, leaving only nine adults, three babies and two ten-year-olds who had escaped into the bush. When he arrived at Derby he handed nineteen children over to the local police, who in turn transferred them to the Beagle Bay Mission. With his task concluded, Isdell declared that it was a strenuous undertaking looking after 'a wild lot of half-caste kids like young kangaroos'.[16]

The zeal to gather in half-castes in the Kimberley did not have sufficient legal backing, a deficiency remedied in amending legislation introduced into the parliament in 1910. In the Legislative Council the Chief Secretary, J. D. Connolly, assumed that there would be wide agreement among his peers that half-caste children should not be allowed to 'continue with the tribes' because in time a 'highly undesirable' state of things would spring up, with a group of 'practically white people' living with the Aborigines.[17] His colleague in the lower house, Mines Minister H. Gregory, explained how essential it was to give the Chief Protector power to 'overrule the mother'. He admitted that

> this may seem harsh, but I am sure those who are familiar with the condition [in the camps] will admit that by this action we are in every sense considering the child itself and are justified in taking this great power.[18]

The new federal administrators who assumed control over South Australia's Northern Territory in 1912 expressed many of the same concerns that had been voiced by their predecessors. Among the many problems confronting the tropical north, the question of the half-caste assumed greater significance in the years before World War II. It was addressed in the two most significant reports provided to the government before 1930 – *The Preliminary Report on the Aboriginals of the Northern Territory* of 1913 by the distinguished scientist and ethnographer Professor Baldwin Spencer, and *The Aborigines and Half-Castes of Central Australia and North Australia* of 1929 by Queensland's Chief Protector of Aborigines, J. W. Bleakley.

Spencer believed there were probably one hundred to 150 half-castes in the north of the Territory and about the same number around Alice Springs. They were, in his view, a very mixed group. While the mothers were Aboriginal in practically all cases, the fathers were European, Chinese, Japanese, Malay or Filipino. The mothers were 'of very low intellectual grade', while the fathers 'most often' belonged to the 'coarser and more unrefined members of higher races'. Consequently, the half-caste was in a 'most unfortunate position', belonging neither to the Aborigines nor to the whites. But one thing was certain in Spencer's mind. The white population as a whole would 'never mix with half-castes'.

What was required was to remove the children in question from the Aboriginal camps. They should all be withdrawn and placed in settlements and on stations. When the children were very young they could be accompanied by their mothers but with older ones the separation should be imposed. Spencer argued that even though it might seem cruel to remove the children it was 'better to do so' when the mother was living in a camp. While in exceptional cases young half-castes could be educated or provided with land for farming, the majority should be confined on reserves and be encouraged to marry among themselves. Girls presented a particular difficulty. The experiment of bringing them up among the whites was fraught with danger, owing to the 'temperament of the half-caste' and to the fact that no white man would marry one.[19]

If anything, Bleakley was more concerned than Spencer about half-castes. It was the 'most difficult problem of all to deal with'. There was the question of what to do with 'those now with us' and, even more significantly, the problem of 'how to check the breeding of them'. Given the conditions of life in the Territory and the absence of white women, the 'evils of miscegenation' would in all probability continue. If only European women would face the 'hardships of the outback' the situation would be much easier to manage. One good woman in a district, Bleakley believed, would have more restraining influence than all the Acts and regulations.

Bleakley's policy prescriptions were similar to those pursued by his own administration in Queensland. All half-castes of illegitimate birth should be 'rescued from the camps' and placed in institutions for care and training. Even when a child was being maintained by the putative father, admission to an approved institution 'should be insisted upon'. When rescued from the camps and provided with education and rudimentary vocational training, the half-caste could be made an asset to the Territory. Left in their existing position, they were more likely to be a menace. The increase of the quadroon element would be 'an even more deplorable result'.

Bleakley believed that half-castes should be allowed to remain part of the Aboriginal community and be 'raised to this civilization' in company with the young Aboriginals of their own generation. He dealt with suggestions current at the time that separate colonies be set up for 'all crossbreeds of aboriginal blood' and that they be segregated from both whites and blacks. He believed that such settlements would fail, eventually creating 'a second colour problem likely to prove troublesome in later years'. The advice he received from all classes of persons with 'experience in dealing with aboriginal half-castes' was that people with 50 per cent or more Aboriginal blood, 'no matter how carefully brought up and educated', would drift back to the Aboriginal society and an atmosphere congenial to them. There was no point in trying to separate them.

Lighter-coloured mixed bloods – quadroons and octoroons – on the other hand should be guided away from Aboriginal society.

Bleakley suggested that children of ten or twelve years, where such could be done without inflicting cruelty on the half-caste mother, should be placed in a European institution where they could be given a reasonable chance of absorption into the white community 'to which they rightly belong'. Institutions in Adelaide would be ideal venues for the project. And the earlier the children could be taken the better, before they had been 'irretrievably leavened with the aboriginal influences'.[20]

The Commonwealth Government laid down the legal structure that would control the Aborigines in the Territory in ordinances passed in 1912 and 1918. They provided the same sort of powers that had been embodied in legislation in Queensland, Western Australia and South Australia. The Chief Protector was given authority to exercise care, custody or control of Aborigines and half-castes. He could take them into custody, control their move-ments, confine them to reserves or prohibit their entry into any defined prohibited area. The protector was the legal guardian of Aboriginal and half-caste children. The 1918 Ordinance, Chesterman and Galligan observed, 'evidenced an administrative preoccupation with miscegenation'. Aboriginal women required special permissions to marry a non-Aboriginal man. It became an offence for a non-Aboriginal to engage in interracial sex.[21] Power was extended to allow the control of quadroons. Half-caste men were liberated from the protector's control on turning eighteen, but there were provisions to place any male under the Ordinance's provisions if in the protector's opinion it was 'necessary or desirable in the interests of the Aboriginal or half-caste to do so'.[22] Women remained under the protector's authority indefinitely.

Despite the zeal to control half-caste children and take them
into care, the conditions in the two institutions – the Bungalow in
Alice Springs and the Kahlin Home in Darwin – were extremely
poor. They were grossly overcrowded. In 1921 fifty-two children
lived in three small iron sheds behind the back fence of Alice
Springs's Stuart Arms Hotel. In Darwin in 1928, sixty-seven children and nine adults were housed in a bungalow originally built
for a single family. Both institutions were poorly equipped and
understaffed, with inadequate sewerage and drainage. A one-time
inmate of the Bungalow recalled in later life the conditions she
experienced:

> It was just concrete floor, no beds, one big shed was built there, and
> a little bit of kitchen on the side . . . We used to get no mattress;
> only blankets to sleep on . . . Two or three girls would get together –
> no pillows, the concrete floor we slept on, you wouldn't even let
> your dog sleep on, it was so rough. Winter time it was freezing.[23]

Despite the official rhetoric about preparing the children for
life in mainstream society, inadequate funding meant that what
education was provided was rudimentary, and even the food supply
was barely enough to maintain the health of growing youngsters. In
his book on the subject Tony Austin recorded the reminiscences of
one-time inmates and many referred to the hunger and the often
desperate search for food. One woman told him:

> We never had any shame about looking into a garbage drum
> for something to eat – we did that often. Now we were virtually

starving, literally starving, which prompted us to steal a good bit. We used to go down and rat the Chinese garden near the Botanical Gardens . . . Breakfast was one slice of bread; you were very fortunate if you got a smearing of jam. And you had to scrounge a fruit tin or some type of tin. You washed that out and kept it; that was your tea pannikin and they sweetened your tea for you. You weren't allowed to sweeten your own because they reckoned you might take too much sugar. That was breakfast.[24]

During the 1920s the federal government faced increasing criticism about conditions in the two half-caste homes. Irate townspeople urged their removal to more remote locations; southern humanitarians were outraged at the failure of the government's duty of care; proponents of White Australia were deeply troubled by the burgeoning population of half-castes at a time when the white population of the Territory was either stationary or declining. There was a constant stream of articles in the southern newspapers about the half-caste menace. A letter in the *Adelaide Advertiser* in November 1924 was typical of the genre:

There are few questions of greater difficulty and delicacy affecting the Northern Territory than the condition of half-caste children and others of mixed parentage, the offspring of that sexual relation which civilization always and everywhere condemns, and which is particularly deplorable when it involves the mingling of the blood of white and black races. It is a frequent and, indeed, almost invariable experience that the progeny of such unions combine the defects without the virtues of the opposing stocks thus unhappily blended. The hybrids, doomed too often to a life of vagabondage, constitute a more serious problem than the blacks themselves.[25]

Prominent and widely read journalists like M. H. Ellis and Ernestine Hill joined the chorus of alarm. Writing in the *Daily Telegraph* in 1924, Ellis warned his readers that in the north White Australia was a myth. It was a half-caste realm where the blood of half a dozen nations mingled in 'a sinister human broth'. As well as pure Australian natives and Asians there was the hybrid that haunted 'every wood heap' and which was even more horrible 'because often it is so nearly white that one cannot tell it from pure British stock, except for its rheumy, black-fellow's eyes'.[26] In a similar vein Ernestine Hill declared that the overwhelming problem of northern Australia was the steadily increasing propagation of a half-breed race. Under a picture of a 'Half-caste mother and her quadroon baby', Hill wrote:

> Unrecognised by his father and unwanted by his mother . . . he is the sad and futureless figure of the north – half-caste.
>
> Child to a tragedy far too deep for glib preaching, half-way between the stone age and the twentieth century, his limited intellect and the dominant primitive instincts of his mother's race allow him to go thus far and no further.[27]

CHAPTER 10

Breeding Out
the Colour

Anxiety about half-castes peaked during the 1930s and was most pronounced in Western Australia and the Northern Territory, where Aboriginal policy-making was dominated by two powerful and determined Chief Protectors – Dr Cecil Cook in the Territory and Aubrey Octavius Neville in the West. Though working quite independently of each other, they devised policies that had much in common, while they shared the same anxieties about the future and similar convictions that immediate remedial action was necessary to safeguard the future of White Australia.

Cecil Cook became Chief Protector of Aborigines in the Northern Territory in February 1927 and retained the post until 1939. He was also Chief Medical Officer and Quarantine Officer. He was twenty-nine years old when appointed and already an expert in tropical medicine. He was undoubtedly the best-qualified person to supervise Aboriginal affairs in northern Australia in the inter-war years. The Northern Territory historian Tony Austin believed that during the late 1920s and '30s Cook exercised 'a towering dominance in Aboriginal affairs' but points out as well that the whole administration of the Top End was poorly funded and was wholly dependent on decisions made in far-off Canberra, where other and competing influences were often paramount.[1] Cook was better informed about and more interested in Aboriginal matters than many lacklustre predecessors. He was also highly authoritarian and supremely confident in his ability to utilise his expertise. Austin observed that one of his very first acts as protector was to implement a system of censorship of films before they could be viewed by Aborigines.[2]

Cook's obvious concern and interest manifested itself in what Austin described as a crushing paternalism. He greatly increased the number of children brought into the institutions in Darwin and Alice Springs and tightened control over the lives of adults.[3] The Aboriginals Ordinance of 1927 amended the definition of 'Aboriginal' to allow control of any half-caste man over twenty-one who in the opinion of the Chief Protector was 'incapable of managing his own affairs'. Prior to 1924 half-castes had become free of bureaucratic control at the age of eighteen. This was extended to twenty-one in that year.[4] In justifying this massive extension of power, Cook wrote:

In certain instances adult male half-castes under Chinese or other influences become the victims of gambling habits, alcohol and opium. Their money is squandered very shortly after its receipt and they are in consequence exposed to temptations and are likely to become a menace to the peace of the community.[5]

A further ordinance in 1933 made it an offence for any male other than an Aborigine or half-caste to consort with an Aboriginal woman unless lawfully married in a ceremony sanctioned by the protector.[6]

Like Neville in the West, Cook was deeply committed to a White Australia. He was a firm believer in the capacity of Europeans to settle in the far north and in the importance of public health measures to facilitate that development. In his annual report of 1937 he explained the need for the maintenance 'in its inviolability of the national policy of a White Australia'. It was, he declared, something that the Australian people regarded as sacrosanct. 'All States, all political parties', he wrote, and all sections of the people were united 'in an ardent desire to maintain racial purity'.[7]

Half-castes presented Cook with a complex and difficult problem. In absolute terms their numbers weren't great, but in relation to the small white community they were demographically significant. While reporting on his year's work in 1931 Cook observed that the half-castes approximated in number to one third of the European population and their rate of increase was much higher than any other section of the population.[8] In that year there were 2950 Europeans in the Territory and 852 half-castes. But, as Cook explained to Administrator R. J. Weddell, the white population was actually declining by 1 per cent annually while the half-caste community was increasing by 2 per cent. The half-caste population was much younger than the European. The implications were clear. If the existing trend continued, the half-castes would become the predominant part of the local population in fifteen or twenty years.[9]

But it was not numbers alone that exercised the mind of the

young protector. He was equally concerned about the rich racial and ethnic mixture in the Territory, especially the number of part-Asian Territorians. Cook did not initiate this obsession. His predecessors had also looked with disdain on Darwin's polyglot population and sought to prohibit sexual relations between Aboriginal women and Asian men. Acting Protector W. L. Fothergill reported in 1930 that action was being taken to discourage any associations calculated to result in or encourage such interracial marriages.[10] Cook was even more emphatic. Previous uncontrolled sexual activity had resulted in a 'hybrid coloured population of a very low order'. He was, he wrote, unable to speak for Queensland and Western Australia, but these coloured individuals constituted a perennial economic and social problem in the Territory, so much so that their 'multiplication throughout the north of the continent' would be attended by 'very grave consequences to Australia as a nation'.[11]

Sensitivity in the Territory's administration about racial mixture was illustrated by reports of the late 1920s and the '30s. These analysed the racial provenance of children in public schools in minute detail and carefully monitored the percentage of Europeans in the mix (see tables 3 and 4 overleaf), fearing that any increase in the number of half-castes among the student body would inevitably result in a 'lowering of the general standard of education for all children in attendance'.[12] The Education Branch's annual report for 1932 counted 179 Europeans in public schools – 151 British and twenty-three Greeks. There were sixty-eight Chinese and two Afghans. But the others were remarkably mixed. There were seventy-eight European–Aboriginal half-castes and then

European–Malays, Chinese–Aborigines, Malay–Chinese, Malay–Aborigines and twenty-two children who were described as being the offspring of two half-caste parents.[13] The fine, almost obsessive analysis of racial origins reached a high point in the Northern Territory's Annual Report for 1937,[14] with both raw numbers and percentages provided to two decimal points.

The prognosis, Cook decided, was not good for the north. Unless changes were made and made quickly, the half-caste population would remain ignorant, indolent, unemployed and destitute. In that condition the whole community would, he believed, provide 'a profitable field for revolutionary agitators' and be numerically sufficiently strong to threaten the 'peace, order and good government of the Territory'. If, on the other hand, the half-caste was encouraged to enter freely into the workforce he would compete as cheap labour and eventually drive out white labour, displacing the Europeans from the Territory with ever-increasing rapidity. Cook feared that the half-caste would 'in his turn displace the white from employment as the white has already displaced the oriental'.[15]

Much, then, was at stake. Either the half-castes would remain outside the economy and become dangerously politicised or they would monopolise the labour market and threaten even further the viability of a white north. From either of these outcomes, Cook observed, only grave disturbances could follow for that part of Australia, which was at once the most sparsely populated and the most vulnerable. The future was, indeed, 'full of menace'. The national ideal of a White Australia was under threat and as things stood it might have to be 'superseded by modification permitting a coloured north'.[16]

Racial Descent of Children on Roll, June 1937

Racial Descent	Schools									
	Darwin	Parap	Pine Creek	Katherine	Alice Springs	Tennant Creek	Kahlin (Half-caste)	Alice S. (Half-caste Instit)	Correspondence	TOTALS
European: (a) British	69	18	10	4	50	24			36	211
(b) Greek	4									4
(c) Russian				1						1
Chinese	60	2		11						73
Octoroon								3		3
Quadroon	6	10		1	12	3	3	14		49·
Half-caste: (a) European – Aboriginal			1				28	50	1	80
(b) Chinese – Aboriginal							3			3
(c) Half-caste – Half-caste	27	3		3		3	1	12		49
(d) Indian – Aboriginal				2						2
Malay – Half-caste	1	2								3
Malay – Chinese	4									4
Aboriginal – Half-caste		2			2			2		6
Cingalese – Half-caste	1						2			3
Afghan – European					2					2
Afghan – Half-caste Afghan					2					2
Half-caste Chinese – Half-caste Aboriginal					3					3
Half-caste Chinese – Aboriginal					2					2
British – Greek	1									1
Japanese – Chinese	2									2
Chinese – Greek	1									1
European – Asiatic	3									3
Indian						1				1
Totals	179	37	11	22	73	31	37	81	37	508

Racial Descent of Children on Roll for June 1937 – Percentages

Racial Descent		Correspondence and Public Schools	Half-caste Institution Schools	All Schools
European:	(a) British	54.36)		41.53)
	(b) Greek	1.02) 55.63		.78) 42.3
	(c) Russian	.25)		.19)
Chinese		18.71		14.37
Octoroon			2.54	.59
Quadroon		8.2	14.4	9.64
Half-caste:	(a) European – Aboriginal	.50)	66.10)	15.74)
	(b) Chinese – Aboriginal	0.00)	2.54)	.59)
	(c) Half-caste – Half-caste	9.23) 10.23	11.00) 79.64	9.64) 26.36
	(d) Indian – Aboriginal	.50)	0.00)	.39)
Malay – Half-caste		.75		.59
Malay – Chinese		1.02		.78
Aboriginal – Half-caste		1.02	1.69	1.18
Cingalese – Half-caste		.25	1.69	.58
Afghan – European		.5		.39
Afghan – Half-caste Afghan		.5		.39
Half-caste Chinese – Half-caste Aboriginal		.75		.59
Half-caste Chinese – Aboriginal		.5		.39
British – Greek		.25		.19
Japanese – Chinese		.5		.39
Chinese – Greek		.25		.19
European – Asiatic		.75		.59
Indian		.25		.19

One of Cook's initiatives was to supply cheap housing for half-castes in Darwin. He provided a justification of the policy in a detailed memo to the Administrator in February 1932. At the time, half-caste men, women and children lived in close proximity to the 'lowest grade coloured aliens' or in the unemployment camps as comrades of agitators and 'extremists of Communism'. Otherwise, families found inadequate shelter in shacks and humpies where they experienced prolonged penury, dirt, discomfort, inadequate diet, overcrowding and 'indiscriminate intermingling of the sexes'. Cook pressed his case with urgency, warning his superior that:

> [i]t must be recognized that this is a problem of great magnitude requiring immediate attention. These conditions are evolving an immoral, degenerate coloured population which, under the influence of communist agitators, is becoming indolent, embittered and revolutionary. The existence and development of a substantial section of the coloured community along such lines strikes at the very basis of the White Australia policy already gravely threatened here by the prolific fertility of Australian-born Chinese. A section of the community having no respect for the social system is one which the remainder of the community must despise and endeavour to suppress, thereby aggravating the influences already at work towards racial conflict. In a White Australia the existence of a coloured community, whether alien, aboriginal or hybrid, must remain a constant menace socially and economically as long as its numbers (a) fail to conform to White standards; (b) are not accepted as White citizens. Where these conditions are satisfied the fact of colour is, of itself, of no import. The problem of urgency is to adopt a policy which will prompt the fulfilment of these postulates, which once achieved will be followed by that dilution of

colour, which will eventually remove the sole remaining indication of miscegeny.[17]

Like so many of his contemporaries, Cook saw the answer to the problem in curbing the growth of the half-caste community, in limiting the 'multiplication of the hybrid coloured population'.[18] Once again it was a matter of controlling the young women of childbearing age. And in Darwin and Alice Springs, young women outnumbered their male contemporaries by at least two to one as a result of the policy of previous administrations to remove girls while leaving their male contemporaries in the bush. Cook realised that such drastic measures as sterilisation, legalised and compulsory abortion or incarceration would be unacceptable, although each was mentioned in passing. The key was to rigidly control marriages of the young half-caste women. In a report to the Administrator, Cook detailed the steps that needed to be taken to reduce the birth rate of half-castes, including

(a) elimination of the factors contributing to the cohabitation of white men and aboriginal women; and

(b) prevention of association between the excess female half-caste population and the male coloured population.

The alternatives were clear. 'If the propagation of the hybrid is to be controlled', Cook advised, 'either the excess females must be detained for the rest of their lives by the Administration or they must be married to men substantially of European origin'.[19]

In seeking to win over sceptical officials in both Darwin and

Canberra, Cook outlined the advantages of white men marrying half-caste girls, provided they had been 'reared to a moderately high standard' in government institutions. Experience showed, he explained, that the half-caste girl could, if properly brought up, 'easily be elevated' to a standard where the fact of her marriage to a white man would not contribute to his deterioration. And what was more, a large proportion of the half-caste female population was derived from what he called the 'best white stock' in the country. So Cook offered a solution to the half-caste problem that did not require drastic measures. All that was needed, he explained, was

(a)   to refuse coloured aliens permits to marry half-caste females. This has now been the practice in the Territory for some years;

(b)   to elevate the half-caste girl to a high living standard so that there may be no question of her impairing the social or economic status of her husband. Considerable progress has already been made in this direction in the Territory.

(c)   to permit half-caste girls to marry carefully selected whites and by extending the Half-Caste Housing Scheme to assist husbands to provide proper homes.

(d)   to permit it to be generally known that such marriages are not officially opposed and to take such steps as are practicable to overcome any conservative prejudice against them.[20]

Cook did much to improve the health, education and employment conditions of half-castes in the Territory to the extent possible with limited funds. He would have done more if the federal government had provided the resources. He also desired to break down the rigid caste barrier and sought to grant full citizenship rights to selected half-castes. These were radical proposals for their time, Cook describing them as 'modern, humane and advanced' in that they involved the granting of full citizenship to a 'generation of persons who may fairly claim it'. But the long-term objective was to breed out the colour, to improve the life of the Territory's half-castes so they could be merged into the mainstream. He considered them to be 'exceptionally assimilable', holding the view that they had no national outlook, social custom or alien background 'incompatible with full white citizenship'.[21] Cook appreciated the fundamental ambivalence at the heart of his policy, believing that it provided the 'only instrument of realising the objective of the conservative purist who demands an All White Australia'.[22]

Cook framed his policy with a sense of urgency. The apparently inexorable growth of the half-caste population called for immediate action. While it was true that in the mid-1930s the half-caste did not present an immediate national problem, he thought it was 'beyond dispute' that

unless the matter of his propagation be dealt with immediately, Northern Australia will be faced in the course of a few decades with an insuperable problem necessitating the admission of a preponderating number of frankly coloured citizens to full social and economic equality. In those days all the objections to their assimilation which can be raised now would be raised again with infinitely more force but the exigencies of the circumstances would demand that they be over-ruled. In my opinion the only solution to the problem lies in discarding prejudice now whilst the numbers involved are of less significance and there is opportunity of doing so with every prospect of success.[23]

Central to Cook's thinking was a view of miscegenation that at the time was quite progressive. When many in the community were still convinced that half-castes were degenerate and that they inherited the worst qualities of both parental races, he argued that race mixing would bring advantages. The Aboriginal inheritance would, he believed, bring to the hybrid 'definite qualities of value'. Among them he listed intelligence, stamina, resource, high resistance to the influence of the tropical environment and the 'character of pigmentation' which even in high dilution would serve to reduce the at present 'high incidence of Skin Cancer in the blonde European'.[24]

Both Cook and Neville challenged conventional thinking about racial mixture in other ways as well, arguing that it was possible for Europeans and Aborigines to breed without the danger of what were known as throwbacks. They publicised this heterodox view in the daily newspapers at much the same time. In an interview with Ernestine Hill in 1933, Cook announced that there was 'no atavistic tendency' as was the case with 'the Asiatic and the negro'. Generally by the fifth and invariably by the sixth generation 'all native characteristics' of the Aborigines were eliminated. The problem of the half-castes, he predicted, would be quickly eliminated by the complete disappearance of the black race and the 'swift submergence of their progeny in the white'. Cook explained to Hill that the Australian native was the most easily assimilated race on earth, 'physically and mentally'. The quickest way out 'was to breed him white'.[25] In his article 'Coloured Folk' in *The West Australian*, A. O. Neville had much the same message. Atavism was not in evidence so far as colour was concerned. 'Eliminate the full blood', he declared, 'and permit the white admixture and eventually the race will become white'.[26]

The two influential protectors had clearly broken away from much expert – and popular – opinion about the likely consequences of miscegenation. But it was only a partial liberation from established dogma and related quite specifically to what they would have called the European–Aboriginal cross. When it came to other racial groups – Africans and Asians, for instance – they returned to the haven of convention. Neville took the view that his ambition to render the race white was only possible so long as 'the Negro, Malay and other coloured races' were rigidly excluded. His views about Negro blood were quite excessive, even for the time. The slightest trace of Negro blood, he believed, was readily observable and it would require 'but a comparative few to keep the race dark forever'. He thought there was good historical evidence to support his view. Early West Australian settlers had brought African and West Indian servants to the colony who had left their 'distinctive features on our Southern coloured population to a marked extent', and time had not eliminated the strain.[27]

Cook and Neville's policies of biological absorption rested on the assumption that the Aborigines were racially akin to Europeans. Neville was quite clear about this. In his speech to Commonwealth and state protectors in Canberra in 1937 he explained that his 1936 legislation was based on the presumption that the Aborigines 'sprang from the same stock as we did ourselves'. They were 'not negroid, but give evidence of Caucasian origins'. We have, Neville explained, accepted the view in Western Australia.[28] And that may have been the case. It was shared by some of the members of parliament who passed the bill in question. The member for South-West Province, Leslie Craig, argued in the relevant debate that '[t]he natives are of the same blood as we are, and the colour can be bred out of them for the reason they are not like Asiatics or Negroes'.[29]

Behind Craig, Neville and Cook stood the biologists and ethnographers who had, over a period of years, transformed the Aborigine from Oceanic Negro to proto-Caucasian. Throughout most of the nineteenth century, Aborigines were categorised on the basis of skin colour, which placed them in the company of Africans and Melanesians. In an address to a meeting of the Australian Association for the Advancement of Science in Adelaide in 1907, the noted medical scientist W. Ramsay-Smith noted that formerly the Australians were classed with the American Negro because both possessed a 'flat nose, protruding lips, projecting jaws and large-sized teeth'. But in rejecting this interpretation he observed that in 1893 the distinguished senior British scientist Alfred Russel Wallace had concluded that Aboriginal biological links had to be sought in a different direction; that they must be classed as Caucasians. Ramsay-Smith remarked that, speaking popularly, this view established that the Aborigines were racially the uncles of the Caucasians.[30] In 1909 he argued that it had been determined that they were a 'homogeneous race, unmixed in descent, of Caucasian stock, not Negro or negrito'.[31] Drawing together other authorities, Ramsay-Smith noted that the young German scientist Richard

Semon, who had visited Australia in the 1890s, had concluded that the Aborigines were more nearly allied to Europeans than were Malays, Mongols and Negroes.[32] This view gradually gained intellectual support with the British biologist R. Lydekker, writing in 1908 that among scientists the Australians were 'generally considered to be low grade Caucasians'.[33]

The proposition was given added respectability by the German scholar Hermann Klaatsch in his major work published in 1914 and translated as *The Evolution and Progress of Mankind* in 1923. Klaatsch concluded that the Aborigines were 'closely related' to Europeans, which was certainly not the case with the Africans.[34] Herbert Basedow was a student of Klaatsch, a South Australian colleague of Ramsay-Smith and briefly Protector of Aborigines in the Northern Territory. He became one of the most determined proponents of the proto-Caucasian thesis, writing a long letter on the subject to the two Adelaide newspapers in April 1919 in which he declared that the Aborigine was 'our racial brother'. Indeed, the Europeans were of the same 'ancestral stock and have evolved from an ancient Australoid type'. For this reason, he continued,

we cannot in a strictly scientific or racial sense speak of a difference between ourselves and the Australian aborigine as it exists, for instance, between ourselves and the Negroids or the Mongoloids. Modern research . . . has convinced us that we and the Australian aborigines are extremes in the evolution of one and the same type. For this reason alone we are not even justified in referring to a blood mixture of the two extremes as a bastard. From an anthropological point of view, a child born of an Australian aboriginal mother and a

European father is not a half-caste but represents the union of long separated and differentiated but still of the same strain or caste.[35]

Basedow went further, arguing that the Aborigine was 'not even a black-fellow'.[36] His colour was due to the intensification of sunburn or tan. He returned to the subject in his widely read *The Australian Aboriginal*, published in 1925, and reiterated the argument that modern-day Europeans were representatives of a race that had evolved from the ancient stock that had been isolated in Australian during long ages of dramatic change. The Aborigines stood near the bottom rung of the 'great evolutionary ladder' up which the white man had ascended. Basedow tried his hand at a metaphor – 'he the bud, we the glorified flower of human culture'.[37]

During the 1920s Australian scientists returned to the subject armed with new technologies relating to blood groups. A. H. Tebbutt concluded in 1923 that it was possible to reach the 'tentative inference' that the Aborigines came from the same primitive stock as Western Europeans.[38] Further work on blood groups was carried out by the distinguished South Australian scientist J. B. Cleland, who reported the results of blood tests carried out on 678 Central Australian Aborigines to a meeting of the Royal Geographical Society in Adelaide. His conclusion was that the Aborigines represented the pure strain that was dominant in the early Europeans and they were therefore more closely akin to white man than 'the Chinaman or the Negro'.[39]

CHAPTER 11 | 'A Colossal

Menace'

During the 1930s, West Australian politicians and officials alike fretted about the rapid growth of the half-caste population, particularly in the southwest. Anna Haebich estimated that between 1930 and 1934 roughly 600 articles and letters relating to Aborigines appeared in Perth newspapers, while between July and August 1933 the government received 150 representations concerning the situation in the southwest.[1] The figures presented to parliament provided dramatic evidence of rapid demographic change. The half-caste community was growing, the population was youthful and many families had large numbers of children. Between 1917 and 1925 numbers had spiralled from 1600 to 4245. While children made up only 16 per cent of the full-blood population they were just under 48 per cent of the half-caste community.[2] Clearly the prospect was for continued rapid growth.

In parliament in 1936 Leslie Craig, a member from the southwest, observed that the half-caste number would soon be 40 000 instead of 4000 and the problem would then be out of control.

Indeed, he believed the 'breeding of half-castes' constituted a 'colossal menace to the State'.[3] G. B. Wood thought likewise. Referring to the latest population estimates, he remarked that so fast were 'these people breeding' that there would be so many half-castes and coloured people in the State that they would not know what to do. 'But we owe it to the future generations of white people', he asserted, 'that something should be done to stop this ever-increasing menace'.[4]

Wood's colleagues were in general agreement. Half-castes were trouble. Vernon Hammersley observed that it had always been recognised that they got to 'know rather too much'. They were, another member declared, 'a less desirable person' than their Aboriginal forebears.[5] The Hon. Sir James Mitchell believed that 'no one wants the half-caste very much', because they were 'neither white nor black'.[6] They were outcasts; they were a tragedy. Wood drew a grim picture of 'the half-caste and quarter-caste' and other blacks of various hues, 'almost all colours of the rainbow living in filthy camps'. Many of them were 'only breeding a race of rotten loafers, good for nothing and nobody'.[7]

The West's politicians had their anxieties confirmed by the Royal Commissioner, H. D. Moseley, who delivered his report on the Aborigines in January 1935. He was both clear and emphatic in his judgement about the half-caste problem. He declared 'without hesitation' that at the present rate of increase the time was not far distant when 'these half-castes', or a great majority of them, would become 'a positive menace to the community; the men useless and vicious and the women a tribe of harlots'.[8]

While the commissioner and the legislators were acutely

aware of the terrible social conditions suffered by the half-caste community – unemployment, poverty, discrimination, inability to gain education – their solution was overwhelmingly a biological one. In the parliamentary debates some members expressed their understanding of and sometimes their compassion for the community's suffering, but their response was to try to control the future growth of the population. Leslie Craig told his colleagues about his experience at a local agricultural show. He had seen many families and was surprised 'at the turn out of the half-castes on that occasion'. They wore clothes that were clean and well ironed. Locals told him that many of the men were good workers and that 'if handled properly' became useful citizens. But even then he was not persuaded, declaring 'the worst feature is the growth of these people'. One farmer informed him that one of his employees was a competent worker 'but had sixteen children'. His informant referred to a neighbour who employed another man who had ten children. 'If this is to occur throughout the country', he warned, 'it will readily be seen what is likely to happen'.

Craig believed that society had a duty to these people, arguing that the whites 'contaminated their blood' and that, therefore, there was an obligation to see that they had an opportunity to earn a living. But to allow this to happen it would be necessary to take the children, and especially the girls, away from their families and to train them in State institutions and to teach them the dangers of sex. 'We should take the girls away from their mothers', he advised, 'when they reach a certain age and train them. They should be removed at as early an age as possible so that their removal will not be too much of a wrench for their mothers'.[9]

It was a prescription that appealed to other honourable members. Alexander Thomson thought that every half-caste child should be taken out of the native camps.[10] G. B. Wood said that he would 'not be above' taking the children away from their mothers 'at the earliest possible stage'.[11]

The answer that many members sought was to be able to control sexual contact, marriage and the birth of children. The most dramatic action suggested was to isolate half-caste from full blood. 'If we can separate the half-castes from the pure blacks', Leslie Craig observed, 'we shall go a long way towards eliminating the colour trouble'. The blending, he declared, must be towards the white. The colour must not be allowed to drift back to the black. In that manner the State would go a long way towards 'breeding the dark blood out of these people'.[12] G. B. Wood put forward similar proposals, telling the members of the Legislative Council that the protector should be instructed to see that no half-caste should be permitted to marry a black. He knew, he said, that the long-distance view was 'to breed these people right out'. But while the half-caste was able to mate with the 'full blacks', the process was being reversed. In five years' time, he warned, there would be many more half-castes and quarter-castes than were currently apparent.[13]

Given the sense of crisis, the belief that the situation was 'full of menace and danger', and the great hostility expressed towards the State's growing half-caste population, it is scarcely surprising that some members of parliament posed the most provocative question of all. E. H. Angelo, member for Gascoyne, asked: '[W]ould it not be better if the race were not perpetuated hereafter?'[14] In a 1929 speech he declared:

There is one question I have often heard discussed, a most important question, on which I certainly should not like to express an opinion or cast a vote in this House without the fullest inquiry. Are the natives and half-castes to be encouraged to perpetuate their race, or should we adopt a suggestion that by segregation their increase should be minimised as much as possible? It might be a drastic step, but let us consider the life of an Aboriginal or half-caste in the future. The life of neither of them would be an enviable one . . . A great many people are of the opinion that we should do our utmost to make the life of the present Aborigines and half-castes as happy as possible, but that we should prevent them from perpetuating their species . . . Are we doing the right thing by allowing the Aborigines to perpetuate their race in a country where their life in future is not going to be happy? The Aboriginal does not want him; the white man does not want him; nobody wants him. The half-caste is unwanted by all.[15]

Few of the sentiments expressed in the parliament would have surprised or troubled the Chief Protector, A. O. Neville, who was in office from 1915 to 1940. He too became increasingly concerned with the half-caste problem and proposed drastic solutions. In his annual report for the financial year 1934–5 he recalled that since 1915 the character of his department's work had gradually changed. When he first took office the half-caste population was in its infancy. Twenty years later, it had assumed formidable proportions and the activities of the department had to be considerably extended to meet ever-increasing needs.[16]

Neville outlined his views on 'Our Coloured Folk' in two long

articles in *The West Australian* in April 1930. He began by emphasising 'the fecundity of the half-caste'. Large families were the rule,
small ones the exception. Unattached women often produced
many children by a variety of fathers. The case of those fathered by
white men was 'sad indeed'. Many of them were beautiful youngsters, 'three parts white, showing barely a trace of black', yet leading
the nomadic life of the Aboriginal and sometimes 'under the control
and tutelage of a full blood or half caste foster father'. It was, he
insisted, not unusual for half-caste and even quarter-caste girls to
be betrothed while still quite young to elderly full bloods.

The half-castes, according to Neville, had little family life,
social place or legal position with either white or black. Their
circumstances fluctuated according to the seasons and overall
economic conditions. When difficulties arose, families wandered
from place to place in search of work. Neville scoffed at his
contemporaries who believed in letting 'these folks work out their
own destiny'. 'What is their destiny?' he asked rhetorically. His
reply was, '[H]ow can an uneducated, untrained, ill-nurtured,
weakly people such as these fight against life as it is today?' And
what chance, he declared, have the children of facing the world
in years to come with no home life, no standards even to guide
them . . . no moral backing to help them in the strong call of sex,
'unmoral, not immoral, because they know no other life or way'.
Neville concluded his first article with the peroration: 'Hundreds
of children are today approaching adolescence. What is to become
of them?'[17] He answered his own question in the first sentence of
his second article published the following day. 'Our coloured folk',
he insisted, 'must be helped in spite of themselves'.

Neville provided a more detailed justification for his policy in evidence given to the Royal Commission in 1934. He observed that in the south of the State a situation had been reached where decisions had to be made concerning the future welfare 'of these people'. They were 'a nameless, unclassified outcast race, increasing in numbers, decreasing in vitality and stamina'. Western Australia was at the parting of the ways. The community had to decide whether it should endeavour to make the half-castes 'useful, self-respecting, law-abiding people' or an outcast race that would rapidly become an increasing incubus on the State. 'Above all things', he declared, 'they have to be protected against themselves, whether they like it or not . . . [T]hey cannot remain as they are'.[18]

To carry out his chosen policies Neville required greater powers than those provided for by the Act of 1905. A bill to bestow them on the Chief Protector was debated but defeated in the parliament in 1929. But in 1936, in the aftermath of the Royal Commission, a new Act was passed and Neville, now known as the Commissioner of Native Affairs, welcomed his expanded authority. The new title was chosen with care because the legislation extended control over almost anyone with any demonstrable degree of Aboriginal blood. Legal guardianship of Aboriginal children was vested in the commissioner, 'notwithstanding that the child has a parent or other living relative'. Control over marriages was expanded. Previously, approval was needed for the marriage of an Aboriginal woman to a non-Aboriginal. From 1936, no marriage of any coloured person could take place without the commissioner's approval. Penalties against interracial sexual relations were increased.[19] While describing the powers given to him by the new Act, Neville explained that he could take 'any child from its mother at any stage of its life' regardless of whether the mother was legally married or not.[20]

The overriding objective was to prevent the return of those half-castes 'who were nearly white to the black'. Under his legislation 'no half-caste need be allowed to marry a full blooded aboriginal' if it was possible to avoid it.[21] Half-caste children should be absorbed in the general community. In order to do this, Neville explained,

> we must guard the health of the natives in every possible way so that they may be as physically fit as possible, the children must be trained as we would train our own children . . . The stigma at present attaching to half-castes must be banished.[22]

Neville combined a clear concern with the actual conditions of children living in Aboriginal camps and a desire to ameliorate them – certainly beyond the means that were ever at the disposal of his poorly funded department. But there was much more involved than a traditional social welfare agenda. In an interview he gave to a Perth newspaper in 1932, Neville declared that the contemporary view that Aborigines were inferior was 'nonsense'. There was no insuperable barrier to what he believed was their improvement, their advancement. The native, he declared, should be 'elevated' by means of guidance and protection. And, in the long run, the 'aborigine of Australia' was destined to become 'absorbed in the whites and to emerge as part of the white race'.[23]

Neville left the public service in 1940 but in retirement wrote a widely read book, *Australia's Coloured Minority*, which provided the most detailed account of the intellectual foundation for his erstwhile policies. Given Neville's importance in framing

Aboriginal policy over twenty-five years, the book requires close attention. In his opening sentence he declared that Australia's population included nearly 30 000 people of mixed white and Aboriginal descent – commonly called half-castes, regardless of the actual nature of the mixture. The term was useful because it reminded his contemporaries that it was common to divide the population into Australians proper (that is, he remarked in an aside, 'our white selves'); full-blood Aborigines; and thirdly the 'Aboriginal castes or mixed bloods' who in thought and social behaviour were not yet 'of us' despite the fact that they were 'in our midst and partly of our blood'.[24] They were also half-castes in the sense that they were partly in and partly out of society.

Neville was sharply aware of the strength of the caste barrier that had developed during the 1920s and 1930s and which was 'almost impossible . . . to break down'. Writing of his experience in the State's southwest, he observed:

> They sense, and indeed are made to see, that they are not wanted within the compact residential areas of a town; their place is in the straggling parts, especially if the houses are so dilapidated that whites will not rent them. Apart from this they must build humpies on the town common near the rubbish dump or on the river bank.[25]

Because they lived in these wretched circumstances they were 'looked at askance' by the 'ruling or white class'. Half-caste children were driven out of the public schools by direct action of white parents and in town after town 'representative opinion' urged the government to break up the fringe camps and force the residents onto isolated reserves. All in all, the coloured minority was excluded from 'the amenities and graces of life'.

Neville's solution was biological assimilation. The mechanics of the process had been initiated in Western Australia following the passage of the 1936 legislation. Full bloods should only be allowed to marry other full bloods. In fact, they should be 'rigidly excluded from any association likely to lead to any other union'.[26] And eventually they would die out. What was of greater importance and danger was the possibility that the coloured minority would eventually achieve a sort of homogeneity and, in the process, become a separate ethnic group. It was emphatically an end to be eschewed.

A critical element of assimilation policy was the removal of half-caste children. Until they were trained 'apart from their parents no real progress towards assimilation' was to be expected. 'You will have a struggle to get the children away', Neville confessed, but he was convinced that the parents would eventually be grateful for what had been done.[27] And once the child was removed it must 'never return to live with its parents within a settlement'.[28] Quadroons or 'nearer whites' must be sent as soon as possible to institutions for white children 'and learn to forget their antecedents' while their parents and coloured relatives should be 'strictly excluded from any contact whatever with them'.[29] The reasons for this prohibition were quite clear. 'Take the child in its infancy', Neville explained, 'and it will grow up as you choose to train it'. The child's antecedents would have no influence on its life, 'being completely forgotten'.[30] And the authorities must be persistent to the point of ruthlessness. 'You must for a generation or more pursue this course', Neville declared, 'if you are to do any good'.[31]

For a brief moment at the end of his career the West Australian became a figure of national importance, playing a leading role in the conference of Commonwealth and state Aboriginal authorities held in Canberra in 1937. Neville was able to convince his colleagues to adopt the policy of assimilation nationwide that he had developed in his State during the 1930s. In his speech to the conference he explained that his plans had the long-term objective of merging the two races. And if the coloured people were to be absorbed into the general community, they had to be thoroughly fit and educated. If they could read, write, count, know what wages they should get and how to enter into agreements, that was all that should be necessary. Once that was accomplished there was no reason in the world why they should not be absorbed into the community. To achieve this end, it was essential to have charge of the children at the age of six. It was useless to wait until they were twelve or thirteen.[32]

Half-caste girls were critical to the success of the grand endeavour. They must be prevented from marrying back into the Aboriginal community. Our policy, he explained,

> is to send them out into the white community, and if the girl comes back pregnant our rule is to keep her for two years. The child is then taken away from the mother and sometimes never sees her again. Thus these children grow up as whites, knowing nothing of their environment. At the expiration of the period of two years the mother goes back into service. So that it really doesn't matter if she has half a dozen children.[33]

Neville moved the motion that was adopted by the conference as the agreed national objective of Aboriginal policy:

That this conference believes that the destiny of the natives of Aboriginal origin, but not of full blood, lies in their ultimate absorption by the people of the Commonwealth and it therefore recommends that all efforts be directed to that end.

That the details of administration, in accordance with the general principles agreed upon, be left to individual States, but that there shall be uniformity of legislation as far as possible.

That subject to the previous resolutions efforts of all State authorities should be directed towards the education of children of mixed Aboriginal blood at white standards, and their subsequent employment under the same conditions as whites with a view to their taking their place in the white community or on an equal footing with the whites.[34]

Neville's concern about the people belonging to what he called Australia's coloured minority was genuine and clearly apparent. He wished to improve their circumstances and to end the discrimination that they faced throughout their life. But he didn't want the minority to grow larger or to develop any distinctive political consciousness. Ultimately, he wanted them to disappear. That was the solution to the problem of white racial prejudice – to change the persecuted, not the persecutor. He challenged his colleagues with the same question posed by E. H. Angelo in the West Australian parliament eight years earlier:

Are we going to have a population of 1,000,000 blacks in the Commonwealth, or are we going to merge them in our white community and eventually forget there were any Aborigines in Australia?[35]

To modern ears this sounds like an extraordinary statement. We need to recall that it was made at the first national gathering of state and Commonwealth experts and bureaucrats and that Neville's speech prefaced a motion about policy that received unanimous support. It is clear that Neville meant exactly what he said. It was more than mere rhetoric and can be seen as both the culmination and the epitome of policy-making in Australia from before Federation. We can distinguish the desire to absorb people of mixed descent in one way or another, to fulfil the imperative needs of a homogeneous nation without visible and assertive minorities, and of a uniformly White Australia.

We should also recall the ideas that were current at the time and that were publicly, confidently and unapologetically voiced by politicians, administrators and assorted experts and commentators. One and all had talked of the 'half-caste menace' that they proclaimed was, variously, a 'positive', 'increasing' or 'colossal' menace to the state, to society, even to civilisation. They felt no need for restraint when saying they didn't want to see any more 'half-blooded people born into this world', when they advocated 'the elimination of these people of lighter caste', the breeding of them 'right out', the need to 'prevent them from perpetuating their species'. And then there were those who spoke in ways both enigmatic and deeply sinister about 'finality'. In the most important national report prepared between Federation and World War II, J. W. Bleakley, the pre-eminent administrator of Aboriginal policy, discussed ways 'to check the breeding of them'.

PART 3

Absorption and Assimilation in the Post-war Period

CHAPTER 12

The Caste

Barrier

When the state and federal policy makers met in Canberra in 1937 they clearly showed their concern about the half-caste problem, but it is surprising what little detailed ethnographic information they had at their disposal. Much of the anthropological scholarship conducted up until that time had been directed towards tribal people living in traditional ways in remote areas of the continent. These were the people who, it was thought, could provide information about the putative childhood of the race, about human origins and beginnings and who were rapidly disappearing. But from the late 1930s, anthropologists and journalists began to seriously examine the communities of mainly mixed-descent people living on the fringes of settled Australia in town camps, on government reserves and pastoral stations.

One of the most interesting observers was Paul Hasluck who, as a journalist on the *Western Australian*, wrote a series of articles about the southwest of the State that was published as a pamphlet entitled *Our Southern Half-Caste Natives and Their Conditions* in

Perth in 1939. It was prefaced by the remark of the Royal Commissioner H. D. Moseley, who observed in 1934 that the 'conclusion was irresistible' that the great problem confronting the community was 'that of the half-caste'.

Hasluck began his study with the question of numbers, observing that in 1901 there were 951 half-castes in Western Australia. By 1935 there were 4246. Under a photograph of a family group with four young children he placed a caption that read: 'Rising Numbers – Still They Come'.[1] He noted in the Great Southern district families of eight, nine or ten and up to fourteen children were the usual thing. In one camp he saw a woman who had five children under six and was expecting another. Fifty per cent of the population were children, compared with only 27 per cent in the Australian population as a whole. The children, he thought, caused most alarm but equally gave ground for strongest hope. He declared that:

> Today they are all swarming about the native camps without proper care. Many of them – laughing, ragged urchins, keen in intelligence – are almost white and some of them are so fair that, after a good wash, they would probably pass unnoticed in any band of whites.[2]

But very few of them were going to school and they lived in makeshift housing without water or sewerage on the outskirts of country towns or on dedicated, often derelict, reserves. They had little chance but to grow up as anything but 'gypsy-like outcasts'.

Hasluck appreciated that by the 1930s the mixed-descent communities were largely intermarrying among themselves or with the surviving full bloods. And this concerned him. Colour was not being bred out. In fact, more was coming in. Looking at them with the eyes of what he termed 'a social herd master' seeking to breed up the herd, there appeared to be only one answer – the next generation must be made better, not worse.[3] And that required that the poverty and deprivation which clearly moved the sophisticated young urban journalist had to be attended to.

But Hasluck's concern was larger than remediation of serious social problems. The first question, he declared, was whether the half-caste was going to live inside or outside the community – whether they would always be a separate caste or be assimilated into mainstream society. On the one hand, there would be an ever-expanding, discontented band of people on the fringes. This seemed to be the worst possible scenario. What satisfaction, he asked, would there be in centuries to come in the spectacle of a strictly isolated group of 'foreign' people 'multiplying themselves on biologically unsound lines, going on and on without getting anywhere'. The alternative was to make plans for the gradual reception of the half-castes as individuals and families into the community. This would require the immediate provision of schools and settlements where the children could be prepared for absorption. And while it might mean some immediate expense, the result would be the passing into the community of hundreds of valuable workers and the provision of opportunity to a submerged people. And, more to the point, in two generations 'there should be no half-caste problem'.[4] At the conclusion of his pamphlet, Hasluck observed:

Whatever is done, it should be done at once. The conditions now existing are a reproach to the State, an outrage to human beings and a waste of material. *If there are any feelings of humanity in the*

community, the present order of things will not be allowed to con-
tinue. If we recognise the claims that these people have on us by
blood relationship, we will lift them up instead of pushing them
back to the blacks. If we remain indifferent to that appeal, we cannot escape the fact that we are faced with an embarrassing
nuisance which grows worse every year. The half-caste problem
calls for an immediate solution.[5]

The growing interest in mixed-descent communities within
Australian academic and scientific circles in the 1930s found its
most significant expressions in a joint project of Adelaide and
Harvard universities carried out by the American physical
anthropologist J. B. Birdsell and the Adelaide ethnographer
N. B. Tindale. By Australian standards of the time, it was an
extremely well-funded exercise. The two researchers travelled over
16 000 miles by car in all states over fourteen months, interviewing
and examining 2500 people.[6] The objective of all this endeavour,
Tindale observed, was to grapple with the problem of racial mixture in Australia as a whole. In explaining the background to the
investigation, Tindale wrote that in 1934 the 'plight of mixed
bloods' was a subject of much debate during which conflicting
views tending variously towards segregation and assimilation were
voiced. The harsh economic conditions at the time had impacted
severely on the half-caste community and made their situation
even more precarious. Tindale noted that he

took some part in the discussions and suggested that while certain
evidence tended to support a theory that the interbreeding with

the whites over several generations would enable the mixed bloods to merge with the Europeans without causing material disturbance of the white community, some observers had suggested that this might be an undesirable solution and that taking in an ethnic strain so primitive as that of the Australian aboriginal might be a cause of permanent injury to the 'white' stock.[7]

Tindale concluded that a systematic investigation of the problem of interbreeding of white and Aboriginal people was worthy of serious attention, a conclusion reinforced by travel and consultation in Hawaii and mainland North America. Tindale noted that there were just under 25 000 half-castes in the Australian community and, like Hasluck, he remarked on the high rate of natural increase – or, as he termed it, 'the phenomenal rate of multiplication'.[8] The problem of how to deal with the burgeoning community was 'a difficult but not an insoluble one'.[9] The obvious answer was biological absorption. The two researchers were therefore especially interested in what they called second and third generation crosses. Their situation presaged the future destiny of the whole half-caste community. 'It may be accepted', Tindale explained,

> [t]hat two successive crossings with 'white' blood, the second accompanied by reasonable living conditions and normal education, enables the grandchild of a full-blooded aboriginal woman to take a place in the general community. Where a third crossing with white occurs the children are almost invariably completely merged into the general population.[10]

If Australian governments encouraged the natural process of absorption by positive and planned controls, Tindale wrote, they would minimise the problem and 'in the course of a generation or two, lead to its disappearance'.[11]

The complete assimilation of the half-caste population was then both possible and desirable. But for it to be a convincing proposal, Tindale and Birdsell had to establish that such a 'complete mergence' was biologically safe and could be effected without 'detriment to the white race'. They argued that Aboriginal blood was 'remotely the same' as that of the majority of the white inhabitants of Australia. The Aborigine was recognised as being a forerunner of the Caucasian race and the half-castes were increasingly 'of our own blood', so there was no danger of 'throwbacks' or reversion in later generations to the 'dark Aboriginal type'. After measuring and recording the detailed physical characteristics of 1200 half-castes all around the country, Birdsell concluded that there were no biological reasons for rejecting people with a 'dilute strain of Australian Aboriginal blood'.[12]

Like other assimilationists, Tindale was in favour of dispersing the half-caste communities as widely and quickly as possible. He sought the 'dispersal of all artificial aggregates of mixed bloods'[13] and the radical improvement of the health and education of the whole minority population. The indefatigable researchers had paid particular attention to the living conditions in the communities they visited. The conclusion was that many half-castes were seriously malnourished. The food they obtained only enabled them to function at the lowest levels of vitality 'compatible with survival'. Tindale was shocked by the poverty of the diet available on reserves and missions in many parts of the country. It was often confined to the provision of small amounts of tea, flour, sugar or treacle – barely sufficient to sustain the recipient. 'One result', he wrote, was that such poorly nourished people showed 'little of the joy of living, never, in fact, being properly alive'.[14]

The education available on reserves and missions was equally deficient. Little money was spent on it. Most schoolrooms lacked equipment of any sort. Classes were huge and included children of differing ages. Few of the teachers had been trained and in many cases had other official duties that took precedence over teaching. Where half-caste communities lived in town camps, the availability of education was even more problematic. In many towns right across Australia in the 1920s and '30s, direct action by white parents had barred the access of half-caste children to local state schools. Little wonder then that Tindale's research had led him to the conclusion that in most states there was a high degree of illiteracy among half-castes.[15]

Tindale and Birdsell visited the Tasmanian Aboriginal community in Bass Strait in the summer of 1938–9. The place held particular interest for them. The community had been established on the islands since the early nineteenth century. The racial mixture was more complete there than anywhere else and the local people had an extensive and detailed knowledge of their family histories. The researchers were able to determine the racial origins of every individual to the 64th part. Tindale declared that the community as a whole was 22/64 Tasmanian Aboriginal, 6/64 Australian Aboriginal and 36/64 white. Socially and culturally, too, the researchers believed they had found a community of great interest. They considered that it represented the farthest point on the journey away from Aboriginality.[16] The islanders' mode of life and methods of thinking were 'essentially white' and Tindale thought that in a generation they would lose their identity within the white population of Tasmania.[17]

During the 1940s, students of A. P. Elkin of Sydney University's school of anthropology conducted research in the small rural towns in New South Wales and produced a range of papers on the resident Aboriginal population and on the pattern of race relations. The general picture can be briefly summarised. Although there were clear status distinctions within the Aboriginal communities, the overall picture was one of poverty and deprivation. The majority of people lived on reserves or in town camps that were invariably situated beyond the urban area, on the river bank, out near the rubbish dump, the sewerage depot, the Chinese market gardens or the cemetery.

Housing was characteristically makeshift, composed of cast-off timber, tree branches, flattened kerosene tins, bags and blankets. There was no piped water, sewerage or rubbish collection. The adult men picked up casual work in the local rural industry – fencing, shearing, weeding, horse breaking. Wages were low and irregular. Diet was poor and largely made up of tea, sugar and flour. Marie Reay outlined a typical day's diet for an Aboriginal living in one riverbank camp:

Breakfast: Tea and scones or damper
Dinner: Tea and damper
Supper: Tea and johnny cakes or damper – occasionally saveloys

The diet, she observed, had many deficiencies, notably of eggs, meat, fruit and milk. Tea was drunk without milk and water was used for making scones and damper. Many of the children suffered from bronchitis, pneumonia, general malnutrition, impetigo, sore eyes and a number had rickets. They had no resistance to colds and general epidemics.[18]

In almost all the towns studied during the 1940s and '50s there was a high level of segregation. It was common for Aboriginal children to be banned from the local state school. In her account of colour prejudice at Collarenebri, Marie Reay explained that for many years the children had received little formal education but in 1940 they were admitted to the public school. Within a fortnight the white parents organised a strike. About half the white children boycotted the school. The New South Wales Department of Education agreed to provide segregated schooling and for years the Aboriginal children were taught on the stage of the town hall by an untrained teacher. Reay reported that when the white parents conducted their boycott of classes, they explained their action by reference to the twin concerns of disease and fear of eventual mixed marriage. The second was the most powerful motive. Reay reported the reaction of a labourer's wife who confronted a more tolerant parent who was in all likelihood only a temporary sojourner:

It's all right for you. You're only staying in the town for about two or three years, then you'll be taking your children away. But it's different for us. I don't want my children to grow up with black children and probably marry them.[19]

The hostility to interracial marriage was common in all sections of the white community. Reay observed that middle-class whites were unanimous in their opposition to such unions. White men who married or openly lived with Aboriginal women were regarded as weaklings and traitors to their race.[20]

Almost all the public facilities in all the towns in northern New South Wales were segregated. At the cinemas the Aborigines were required to sit in a roped-off section of seats at the front. However, the degree of stringency and the sanctions marshalled to maintain the situation varied from district to district. In some areas segregation was 'an implicit understanding', in others police were called to evict Aborigines from white seats.[21] Barbers normally refused to cut the hair of Aborigines. If they did so, they would lose their white customers. In some towns the churches effectively barred Aboriginal worshippers. The Anglican Church sought to keep them away from communion because the white parishioners would object to drinking from the same communion cup.[22] If a local doctor accepted Aboriginal patients, he had to see that they entered by a separate door and waited for attention in a different waiting room.[23]

The anthropological studies clearly illustrated the existence of a caste barrier that maintained clear demarcation between white and black. In his study of the New South Wales north coast, M. J. Calley observed that the Aborigine was assigned a place in the social hierarchy well below that of the lowest white man. Writing of the towns in the northwest of the state, Ruth Fink argued that

[t]he adult mixed bloods of today have grown up in a society which looked upon them as the descendants of a primitive race, and which regarded them as incapable of living like white people . . . Those who possess Aboriginal physical characteristics have very little opportunity for social mobility – their colour is a symbol of low status . . . In such a situation, the only way in which coloured people can hope to attain status within the non-coloured group, is by trying to breed out the coloured element through marriage or liaisons with white and lighter coloured individuals. For it is only by ridding themselves of their aboriginal features that they can escape the stigma of the caste barrier.[24]

While the caste barrier was a formidable obstacle in rural New South Wales, it cut a jagged line through society, creating anomalies on either side. Families with little hint of Aboriginality who were known to have indigenous ancestry and who acknowledged darker relatives remained on one side, despite their appearance. Marie Reay wrote of one family who had remote Aboriginal ancestry who were referred to as the 'red-headed black fellows' although they were to all appearances white. A young female family member worked in a local hotel. While Reay thought there was no apparent physical trace of indigenous descent, young men who came to town were warned that she was an Aborigine.[25] There were other families who, arriving from distant settlements, lived in the town maintaining a precarious position as honorary whites. Their situation, Reay believed, was not an enviable one. They found it necessary to work much harder in an effort to win white people's admiration and friendship, while

[m]any of them are afraid of sunburn exaggerating the darkness of their complexions, and as the women grow older they powder their faces more assiduously then ever. One middle-aged woman powders her face many times each day to this end . . . [26]

The studies conducted in various parts of Australia from the late 1930s to the mid-1950s showed in detail the dramatic impact of white racial prejudice. It is an important reminder of what people of mixed descent faced while being encouraged by policy-makers throughout the first half of the twentieth century to break away from Aboriginal kin and communities and merge into wider society. There is no doubt that some did. By moving away from where they were known, by assuming a new identity, they did 'pass' successfully and find a place as white people. Tindale believed that fair-haired part-Aboriginal girls living in the cities passed readily into the general population. He provided a list of individuals who he and Birdsell had come across or heard about in the course of their travels across Australia, noted their caste and their social and economic attainments:

$\frac{5}{8}$ Aboriginal of wealth, married to white woman, attending country dance, or occasion of local golf club celebrations and prize giving.

$\frac{5}{8}$ girl attending an official public ball in a capital city with a white escort and mixing freely with others of her party.

$\frac{3}{8}$ city messenger.

$\frac{1}{2}$ dance band leader supporting a white wife.

$\frac{3}{8}$ girl who has won literary prize in an all Australian competition.

¼   woman cook in white home for twenty years; twice married to whites; son's a sergeant in the second AIF.

½   pastoralist successfully breeding brood horses.[27]

But many other observers of the Aborigines in white society spoke of the rejection, the ostracism and the hostility that placed immovable obstacles in the way of aspiring mixed-descent people. As was often the case, families cut themselves away from their kin to facilitate their acceptance in the white world, only to be rebuffed and humiliated and find themselves isolated and insecure in a racial no-man's land.

There were early intimations of the problems ahead in evidence given to the South Australian Royal Commission in 1913. For all the talk there had been before the commission and in the parliament about absorbing the mixed-blood children, the witnesses with the most direct experience of young residents on the reserves and missions were clear that there was the insuperable problem of white racial prejudice. The community would simply not accept them. W. E. Dalton had been secretary of the Aborigines Friends' Association for more than twenty years. He recalled the experience of the Point Macleay mission that trained young men to be bootmakers at considerable expense. They were then found positions in an Adelaide factory, but after a time only one remained. All the others drifted back to the mission. 'When the native gets among white people', he explained, he is isolated. 'They do not like him; they will have nothing to do with him; and he gets lonely.' If you put a half-caste in the streets of Adelaide, he asked rhetorically, 'how many friends is he going to make among his neighbours?'[28]

T. W. Fleming, the President of Dalton's Association, had much the same story to tell. When asked whether he agreed with the policy of merging the half-castes within the general community he explained that the objection to colour was 'so very strong' that he thought it would never cease to be a difficulty.[29] The Rev. W. J. Bussell, Vice-President of the Aborigines Friends' Association, felt that the task was so difficult that he was opposed to trade training. It was a question of whether the association should encourage too many half-castes to take up trades 'because we do not want to provoke strife'.[30] The commissioners questioned the superintendent of the Point Pierce Mission, F. Garnett, about whether his staff assisted the young half-caste men and women to find employment off the station. He was then asked directly:

> You expressed the opinion that there would be a great difficulty in getting work amongst the white people for native tradesmen. Can you explain what you mean by that?

In reply, Garnett observed:

> White men object to work at trades along with aborigines. The objection to colour comes in, and the aborigines feel it. Even at the shearing sheds . . . the station owners allot one side of the board to the natives and the other side to the white men. It is necessary to separate them for the peace of the workmen. That becomes a practical difficulty in the way of the natives learning trades, such as being carpenters.

His interrogator returned to the general issue, asking whether he based his assumption about the difficulty of mixing black tradesmen among white workers on the situation in the shearing sheds and he replied: 'Yes, and from what I have noticed elsewhere. People do not want the aborigines in trades.'[31]

Mrs J. Matthews, another witness engaged in missionary endeavour, opposed the idea of merging the half-caste population in the wider community. She reminded the commissioners of the ever-present problem of interracial sexual relations, explaining that 'so much unhappiness comes from them mixing with white people'. She related the story of a family who had a 'very nice half-caste girl in their service'. As she grew up, one of the sons wanted to marry her. The mother intervened and sent the young woman back to the mission and the attachment was broken off. Mrs Matthews observed that it would not be wise to encourage such a union and it would have brought a great deal of trouble to the family. She recalled the case of a gardener who began living with a native girl 'but he could not mix with white society afterwards'.[32]

Australia did not witness a slow, even retreat away from racial prejudice during the first half of the twentieth century. All the evidence suggests that it intensified during the 1920s and '30s as the community's commitment to White Australia became more entrenched. This was recognised by some of the very people who were leaders among the influential advocates of absorption. Tindale reported that his half-caste informants were aware of gradually increasing prejudice. They were being faced, he thought, in many places with a new and increasingly intolerant attitude. He thought the influence of American books and films was to blame; Australian attitudes seemed to be tending to increasingly be aligned with the 'general American attitude towards the Negro'.[33]

A. O. Neville, the arch absorptionist, was also keenly aware of the caste barrier. He had seen it first-hand during his career in Western Australia. In retirement he reflected on the fate of many young men and women who had left the reserves and missions and attempted to find a place in wider society. Hundreds of them had returned, he observed, 'defeated by our social ostracism' and 'social rejection of them'.[34] In many instances the 'coloured folk' struggled to improve themselves economically and socially, but they often gave up the struggle. Prejudice, he observed, was 'an almost impossible barrier to break down'.[35] In every aspect of life they were made to feel they belonged to a lower caste. They were 'stared at, jeered at in life and made an object of ridicule in illustrated papers'.[36] Neville followed Tindale in looking to America to understand segregation in Australia, observing that

> [o]ur native people, though never slaves in the same sense as were the American Negroes, are in many respects much less emancipated, in that, unlike the Negro, today they cannot enjoy all the things we enjoy; they are still a people apart. Even when legally free to do as they please, there are reasons why they cannot at present.[37]

Neville's reference to America should remind us that racial questions were international ones of great significance in the middle of the twentieth century. Developments in Australia were influenced by what was going on in the rest of the world. This was particularly so in the years immediately after World War II.

CHAPTER 13 | # Removing Children

There was a growing resistance to racial ideas in many Western countries in the 1930s in response to developments in Nazi Germany. It intensified during and immediately after the war as the full horror of the Holocaust became widely known. In 1948 the fledgling United Nations adopted the Universal Declaration of Human Rights with its equal application to the whole of humanity regardless of race, colour, religion or putative primitiveness. As one of its first tasks the new United Nations Education, Social and Cultural Organization mobilised scholars in many countries to prepare a frontal attack on the concept of race and its application to human biology, anthropology and sociology. This endeavour culminated in two documents: *The UNESCO Statement by Experts on Race Problems* of July 1950 and the *Statement on the Nature of Race and Race Differences – by Physical Anthropologists and Geneticists* of July 1952.

In reporting the first statement on 15 July 1950 the *New York Times* front-page story announced that world scientists had declared race was a social myth and it followed up with a summary of the experts' seven major conclusions:

1. Racial discrimination has no scientific foundation in biological fact.
2. The range of mental capacities in all races is much the same.
3. Extensive study yields no evidence that racial mixture produces biologically bad results.
4. Race is less a biological fact than a social myth.
5. Scientifically, no large modern population or religious group is a race.
6. Tests have shown essential similarity in mental characters among all human racial groups.
7. All human beings possess educability and adaptability, the traits which more than all others have permitted the development of men's mental capacities.

There seem to have been no comparable reports of the UNESCO statement in the major Australian newspapers. Its local relevance may not have been immediately apparent. But so many assumptions that had informed Australian thinking and policy had been undermined. The old ways could not be maintained indefinitely.

The key figure in the reformulation of Aboriginal policy was Paul Hasluck, who we have already met as the author of a series of articles about the Aboriginal communities in the southwest of Western Australia. During the 1940s he was a member of the Department of External Affairs and was involved in the preparatory work for the formation of the United Nations at San Francisco in 1945 and London and New York in 1946. Having resigned from External Affairs in 1947, Hasluck contested and won the West Australian seat of Curtin in 1949 and became Minister for Territories between 1951 and 1961, with responsibility for Aboriginal policy in the Northern Territory and the capacity and ambition to establish national policies and objectives that would unite the relevant state and federal authorities. The first outcome of this coordination was the policy adopted by the Native Welfare Conference of Commonwealth and States in 1951 that declared that the objective of policy was assimilation and the desire to see all persons born in Australia enjoying full citizenship.

Much had changed since the previous national conference of 1937. But much had stayed the same. In 1937 it was assumed that people of mixed descent would be shepherded across a bridge over the wide divide between Aboriginal and White Australia. They would be taken on that journey as children and would be strongly discouraged from ever going back from whence they had come. Ideally, they would never want to return or even know where to return to. Full-blood Aborigines would remain on the far side and would gradually dwindle away until none were left. That was what assimilation meant in the late 1930s. What had changed by the early 1950s was that the expectation that tribal Aborigines would die out had been overturned, or at least could no longer be confidently proclaimed. They too would now travel in the wake of people of mixed descent across the assimilationist bridge, albeit somewhat more slowly and after suitable preparation on the far side. They would not die out. They would eventually be absorbed within the white Australian population.

Much of the new thinking can be illustrated by speeches and statements made by Hasluck himself during the 1950s. In parliament in June 1950 he observed that 'we have on our hands a serious but not a frightening problem'. The Aborigines were a group within but not of the community. Therefore they could be 'and must be managed'.[1] The race relations problem in Australia was softened by the big disproportion in numbers between the two races. There was 'no uncertainty about who will swallow whom'.[2]

Assimilation governed and shaped 'all other native affairs administration'.[3] While speaking to an audience in Melbourne's Wesley Church in 1957 on the subject 'New Hope for Old Australians', Hasluck explained that after many generations the Aborigines would 'disappear as a separate racial group'. The force of numbers was against them. But he hoped and expected that their descendants would carry a 'proud memory of their own ancient origins'.[4] What stood in the way of this result was any form of race consciousness or group identity that threatened the creation of a homogeneous Australia and would facilitate the perpetuation of distinctive minorities.

While Hasluck looked forward to what he thought would be a better future, there were strong elements of continuity linking him with the policies of his Western Australian predecessor, A. O. Neville. Light-coloured children were still removed from parents, kin and community in the Northern Territory and sent to foster homes, institutions and boarding schools in the southern states. While writing of his period in the Territory as a patrol officer with the Native Affairs branch, J. P. M. Long observed that during the 1950s, despite significant reforms, relics of former policies remained and, in particular, the practice of persuading Aboriginal parents of mixed-descent children to consent to their removal to institutions without 'any real examination of the reasons'. Administrators and officials still thought it repugnant to see an almost white child living among Aborigines and this, Long insisted, 'was reason enough to remove the child'.[5]

During the 1950s the Department of Territories introduced a scheme to send mixed-descent children from the Northern Territory to the southern states. It was designed to remove children to be trained, to grow up and ultimately work in an environment that was 'not conscious of the colour problems in the same way the Northern Territory is'.[6] Hasluck believed that transferring light-coloured children out of the Territory was a good policy likely to 'assist our policy of assimilation'. He thought it essential that the transfer should be made 'at an early age'.[7] The expectation was that such children would readily pass as Europeans or readily fit into a European way of life and would find it easier to do so in the south than in the north.

Hasluck provided a detailed explanation and justification for child removals in a response written to a critical letter from an activist in 1951. It is worth quoting at length:

> For many years past under successive governments, the policy has been that, where half-caste children are found living in camps of full-blood natives, they should, if possible, be removed to better care so that they may have a better opportunity for education. The theory behind this policy is, that if the half-caste child remains with the bush tribe, he will grow up to have neither the full satisfaction in life which the tribal native has nor the opportunity to

advance to any other status. This policy is applied with care and discretion and a full recognition on the part of the Administration that the Aboriginal mother has the same affections as every woman. The patrol officers are required, from time to time, to visit the various tribes of full-blood natives and, if it's decided that the advantage of the child will be best served by removal, the patrol officers endeavour to prepare the Aboriginal mother for the eventual separation and to impress her with the advantages which her child will gain. The objective is to have the child willingly handed over to the custody of the Department of Native Affairs and, where possible, the mother is permitted to accompany the child to make the separation more gradual. The purpose of the action taken is to serve the interests of the children and to give them the chance of living at a better standard of life. I have again asked the Administrator to ensure that, in the application of this policy, every care and sympathy must continue to be shown for the natural feelings of the people concerned.[8]

Sister Kate's Home in Perth was a celebrated institution that was specifically set up to take in light-coloured children. After gaining increased powers as a result of the 1936 legislation, A. O. Neville required his field officers to recommend children over two years of age for placement at Sister Kate's as a consequence of their whiteness. In 1946 Aboriginal protectors in pastoral areas were required to provide details of light-skinned children at birth or when discovered for removal to the Perth home. In 1947 the Acting Commissioner of Aboriginal Affairs, C. L. McBeath, indicated that he would not approve of dark-coloured children being admitted to Sister Kate's because it had been established for the education of quarter-caste children 'of true quadroon hue' who, he expected, would be absorbed into the community. While writing to the home's manager he noted:

> As you well realise, dark children could not possibly be absorbed as whites, therefore, it is my wish that every care be taken in the admittance of children in order to ensure that they are fair enough to be regarded as white . . .[9]

In 1949 the superintendent of the home reacted strongly to a magazine article that referred to the institution as a 'half-castes' home'. He wrote to correct the misapprehension, pointing out that Sister Kate's had never had any Aboriginal or half-caste children. They were, he emphasised, all quarter-castes. The home was very sensitive about 'the line of demarcation'.[10]

In 1972 Paul Hasluck as Governor-General spoke to a gathering at Sister Kate's – an institution of which he had been a patron for many years – emphasising that the home had been the refuge for children who nobody wanted or cared for.[11] It had provided an answer to a problem that was social rather than racial. This misreading of what had been the whole rationale for Sister Kate's was symptomatic of the way in which assimilation had been pursued in the 1950s. Although official rhetoric, including Hasluck's own, was all about cultural and social assimilation, ideas about race and colour and blood were still a powerful presence. This is scarcely surprising, given their overwhelming importance in Australia's intellectual and political life during the late nineteenth century and the first half of the twentieth century.

Removal of children from their parents, kin and community that had been central to the very existence of institutions like Sister Kate's had been promoted throughout the history of White Australia, often by people who were convinced they had the best interests of the Aboriginal people at heart. By way of illustration we can turn to two figures, both English immigrants who arrived in Australia seventy years apart – Charles Sturt in 1827 and Auber Octavius Neville in 1897. Both saw themselves (and were regarded by contemporaries) as being sympathetic to the Aborigines. Neville, as we have seen, was for many years the Chief Protector in Western Australia. Sturt was the explorer who wrote sympathetically about traditional society, avoided conflict while in the bush and was a promoter of Aboriginal rights to land as Land Commissioner in early South Australia. Both men wrote books – Sturt in 1849, Neville in 1948. Both advocated the removal of children from their parents and explained their reason for so doing.

Sturt addressed the question of how to prevent Aboriginal children from returning to their families and kin after receiving European schooling. What is to be done? he asked, rhetorically. The question, he realised, was 'involved in difficulty' because the remedy he favoured necessitated 'a violation for a time at all events'

> of all the natural affection, by obliging a complete separation of the child from its parents; but I must confess, I do not think that any good will result from the utmost perseverance of philanthropy, until such is the case, that is, that the children are kept in such total ignorance of their forefathers, as to look upon them as

Europeans do, with astonishment and sympathy. It may be argued that this experiment would require too great a sacrifice of feeling, but I doubt this. Besides which, it is a question whether it is not our duty to do that which shall conduce most to the benefit of posterity. The injury, admitting it to be so, can only be inflicted on the present generation, the benefit would be felt to all futurity.

Sturt hoped that he would not be thought to have the 'character of an inhuman man' but after much consideration his personal experience told him that it was often necessary to adopt a line of conduct we would 'willingly avoid' to ensure a public good.[12]

Almost exactly one hundred years later, A. O. Neville discussed the same question, although he was primarily concerned with mixed-descent or coloured children, every one of whom, he declared, should be placed in a residential school. They must be 'free of all parental control and oversight', must enter the institution at the earliest possible age and 'must be considered to all intents and purposes to be an orphan'. Quadroons 'or nearer whites' must go as soon as possible to institutions for white children and 'learn to forget their antecedents'. Their parents and coloured relatives should be 'excluded from any contact whatever with them'. Once removed, the child must never return to live with its parents. If it did, all the good work already accomplished would be undone. The process did not need repeating ad infinitum but the administrator must pursue this course for a generation or more 'if you are to do any good'. Neville summed up his policy with the memorable aphorism: 'Take the native child in its infancy and it will grow up as you choose to train it, its antecedents influencing its life not at all, being completely forgotten.'[13]

Neville's experience spanned much of the first half of the twentieth century. He began his career in the West Australian public service in 1897 and was Chief Protector of Aborigines from 1915 to 1940. His book was published eight years later. That he should write with such assurance and certainty at the end of his career is a reflection of the views of many of those who exercised power over Aborigines during the decades when the removal of children was seen as the panacea for the half-caste problem.

Children were removed from parents, kin and communities by government agents from the late nineteenth century to the 1960s. They were removed at a much higher rate than white children considered to be in need of care and usually with the authority provided by specific legislation that required neither parental approval nor the sanction of the courts. The disparity between white and black removals would narrow if class was considered and only the poorest 5 per cent of the European community was examined by way of comparison. The actual numbers removed will never be known for certain and remain a controversial question. Robert Manne's cautious estimate of between 20 000 and 25 000 between 1910 and 1970 would appear to be the most acceptable and that would be true also of his assessment that 10 per cent of all Aboriginal children born before 1970 were taken from their parents. If only mixed-descent children were considered, the percentage would be much higher.[14]

The motivation of those directly involved – politicians, bureaucrats, field officers, custodians – has also been much debated. There is no doubt that many children lived in conditions of deep poverty and deprivation. They were often poorly nourished and had no access to health services or education. Even those who were better off were just as likely to be judged by white officials as being in need of care. It is important not to idealise life in fringe camps, on government reserves and cattle stations. But that does not take us to the core of the problem. The demonstrable and indisputable fact is that most children were taken away because they were of mixed descent, regardless of the ambient conditions where they lived. Appearance was everything. Full-blood children were normally left where they were, even while lighter-coloured siblings were taken away.

Participants in the removal process were quite frank about their motivation, as we have seen in earlier chapters. They talked about the disgrace of near-white children living in the camps, about the shame of miscegenation itself. Moral outrage was tinged with horror when young girls were involved. Prurience and censoriousness walked easily together. There was talk too about the need to provide part-white children with a better chance in life, as though through such redemption the shame of interracial sex could be appeased. Mixed-descent children were thought to be more intelligent than full-blood contemporaries and better able to benefit from education and training. Right up until the post-war period it was almost impossible to challenge the assumption that living with white people – even in institutions – was an advance, a step up, almost regardless of the actual conditions likely to be experienced. Anything, it was believed, was better than life in the camps. Such complacent certainty may help explain the often appalling conditions experienced in institutions, foster homes and places of employment.

There can be no doubt that most participants believed in what they were doing and that they felt removal was for the benefit of the targeted children. The policy couldn't have been sustained without that reassuring thought. But what was often misplaced concern about individual children only takes us part of the way to understanding why such policies were implemented. Always in the background, like a distant mountain chain, was anxiety about the nation or, more particularly, about the race. Half-castes, as we have seen, were not merely individuals who exacerbated a perceived social problem; they were also a threat to the idea of a homogeneous White Australia. To miss this part of the story is to totally misunderstand it. And standing behind White Australia itself was the imposing range of racial ideas that dominated scientific and sociological thought in all parts of the Western world before World War II.

But underlying much of the relevant discussions was a layer of unease about taking children away from their mothers. Almost everyone saw that it was an exceptional thing to be doing and inconsistent with normal behaviour. Unease promoted self-justifying explanations. The quickest avenue to righteousness was to claim that Aboriginal mothers didn't care about their children and would soon forget them. More commonly, the view was that while the removal of children was a questionable thing to do and would cause understandable distress to parents and kin, the interests of the child had to be given priority. By the 1950s greater recognition was accorded to the mothers and greater sensitivity was shown to a far more critical public opinion, not just in Australia but overseas as well. As we have seen, patrol officers in the Northern Territory were urged to persuade and cajole parents with persistent advocacy of what benefits would accrue to a child willingly surrendered. Mothers were allowed to travel with targeted children to Darwin or Alice Springs and were sometimes given a photograph as a keepsake.

Once those involved in the practice of taking children were persuaded that it was in the best interests of both the children and society, much else followed as a logical consequence. The follow-through was irresistible. Parental resistance must be overcome, even by force or threat of force if necessary. The younger the child the better before habits were formed, attachments cemented, language learnt, traditions absorbed. The break from family, kin and community must be decisive and permanent, otherwise the whole exercise would be jeopardised. If young people could return to their families the effort had been wasted. That being the case, other aspects of the system made sense even though they appear in themselves to be arbitrary and gratuitous. Children should be provided with no information about where they had come from or where they could return to. They might even be encouraged to think that their parents hadn't wanted them or were dead. Names could be changed to prevent subsequent searches for origin. Siblings were often separated to undermine familial solidarity. Use of tribal language was forbidden on pain of punishment. All memories of an Aboriginal past were to be discredited and allowed to fade away to hasten the cause of assimilation.

None of this was accidental, arbitrary or the result of individual malice. The men and women who shaped and implemented policy knew exactly what they were doing. They were self-consciously important players in the great game of nation building and race consolidation. They were dealing in their way with a problem which at the time was seen as a global one. The assumed gravity of the task blinded them to what they were doing to individuals and communities. There is no doubt they had successes in the terms that they had determined. Some of those mixed-descent children who were abducted and then shepherded across the bridge of assimilation did cast off their Aboriginal heritage, made a go of it in white society and never wished to return from whence they had come. By and large, they did merge into the wider world and we know little about what happened to them thereafter. That was an inevitable consequence of 'passing'.

This question had been little studied until the 1990s. The historian of the stolen generations, Peter Read, argued in 1999 that as many as 50 000 Australians did not identify as Aboriginal but were entitled to because their parent or grandparent had been removed. He believed that the consequences of non-identification by descendants of removed people, due to their lack of knowledge or shame in admitting the fact, had been much underestimated.[15]

What we now know about are the disastrous consequences for large numbers of people that followed from the policy of child removal. During the 1990s hundreds of victims spoke out about their experiences. They can be found in government reports;[16] in oral history collected by Aboriginal organisations,[17] individuals and the National Library; in the work of historians and political scientists;[18] and in numerous memoirs written by people who were subjects of the policy.[19] The report of the Human Rights Commission *Bringing Them Home* was the most comprehensive document drawing on the oral testimony of 535 respondents and another 1000 written submissions. The chairman of the inquiry, Sir Ronald Wilson, observed that in general terms 'each of those stories was corroborative of the substance of all the others'.[20]

The main themes of this large body of literature are clearly delineated and relatively well known. The actual removal of children caused great trauma both to the children who were abducted – or for those old enough to know what was happening – and for parents, for kin and for whole communities. There are many harrowing stories of desperate struggles over children who were literally torn from the arms of their relatives. Lorraine Siwers of the Barunga–Wugulark community was taken from her people in September 1948. She recalls:

> I just saw two men in khaki and they were the ones that came with us on the truck. Mum was trying to hang onto me, pull me, but there was a couple of fellas there putting us on the truck. They were just taking us off our mothers. A lot of them were just screaming. The ladies and old people were by the truck and they were all crying.

The seven-year-old Lorraine did not initially realise the gravity of the situation and thought she was only being taken for a ride. But she came to realise later it was a life-changing moment. She never saw her mother again.[21]

In some cases children were removed from schools and hospitals. In his memoirs Banjo Clarke explained that his wife Audrey was a teacher's assistant at the Framlingham mission school and children were often taken from class and driven away by the 'welfare people'. The children were terrified. Their screams for their parents were to 'haunt many of the Old People until their dying day'.[22] Another informant observed how the impact of the removal of children affected the extended families in question. 'Our grandfather', he explained, was devastated 'when he seen that we all got sent away. It broke his heart'.[23]

For the distraught adults the loss of their children often had severe long-term consequences. Some parents literally never recovered from their loss; many often spent years fruitlessly trying to find out where their children had gone. Those who were able wrote letters to government departments or tried to communicate with their children. They were rarely able to maintain contact, nor were they able to have their children returned. Whole communities were shown in the most brutal and explicit way that they were utterly powerless in the face of white authority.

Children were often taken on long journeys by total strangers with no idea where they were going and why they had been abducted. The new life waiting for them was often one of impoverished institutional existence with overcrowded dormitories, inadequate food, hard work and rigid disciplines. Eileen Mosley, who was removed from her family in the Northern Territory, recalled the life she knew in St Mary's Anglican Hostel in Alice Springs. It was very regimental, she explained:

> You know, everybody got up at the same bell. Bell used to go off to tell us it was time to get up. And it was quite early in the morning,

because as, we had to, you know, prepare breakfast, make our beds, sweep the dormitory and mop the dormitory before we went to school.[24]

Another ex-inmate recalled that it was just like a 'mini army for kids' because it was always strict and there was never any affection.[25]

This was another recurring theme in the testimony of the stolen generation – the sense of being cut off from parental affection, of being uncertain about origins and identity. John Wood, who was brought up in a Salvation Army home before being sent to other institutions and foster homes, recalled:

I had no concept of family life whatsoever really. You know, you moved from one place to another and you're never, never told that you're loved. Nobody ever. I never heard the word, never heard it.[26]

Another witness who gave confidential evidence to the HREOC inquiry confessed that he had 'always been sort of on the outside of things'. He had always had his guard up, 'always been suspicious and things like that'.[27]

The decision to remove children from their communities when they were young and make the break both complete and permanent left many of them uncertain of where they had come from and who they were. In his account of his life given to Carmel Bird, Paul explained:

I had no identity. I always know I was different. During my school-
ing years, I was forever asked what nationality I was, and I reply
'I don't know'. I use to be laughed at, and was the object of jokes.
I would constantly withdraw; my shadow was my best friend.[28]

Another informant reported to the National Library's *Bringing
Them Home* oral history project that as a child he didn't know who
he was. 'I just knew I was a boy', he explained. 'I didn't know I was
born from a mother. I thought I came down from heaven'.[29] Eileen
Cummings from the Barunga–Wugulark community summed up
her sense of what it had meant to be taken away:

I suppose they thought education would compensate but it didn't.
Education doesn't replace the hurt and not having a mother and
not having a family. I'm no better off because I missed out on the
most important things. We missed out on our culture and our
family. Nothing can replace that.[30]

The governments involved in taking children away gave little
indication that they took at all seriously their consequent duty of
care. What education was provided was aimed at producing
unskilled workers – farm hands and domestic servants mainly.
This was true of practically all institutions. All Aboriginal children
were assumed to require the same level of schooling and all would
enter the lowest level of the workforce. But even this minimalist
experiment in absorption faltered against the barrier of white
prejudice. White society couldn't deliver what had been implicitly
promised during the whole era of assimilation. Anyone who looked

Aboriginal was treated with amused condescension or active hostility. One way out was to do everything possible to pass as a dark-skinned European. The other was to find the way back to kin, country and community – to cross back over the assimilationist bridge.

For many mixed-descent people, neither option was possible or appealing. Government intervention had wrenched them out of secure positions in complex and comforting webs of kinship and made of them what they were already thought to be – half-castes caught between two worlds. This situation was mentioned by numerous people who recently provided accounts of their life. One informant told the *Bringing Them Home* inquiry: 'You spend your whole life wondering where you fit. You're not white enough to be white and your skin isn't black enough to be black either.'[31] A second respondent observed: 'You hear white fellas tell you you're a Black fella. But Black fellas tell you you're a white fella. So you're caught in a half-caste world.'[32]

In her life story *Very Big Journey*, Hilda Jarman Muir wrote of her incarceration in the Kahlin Half-caste Home, having been brought to Darwin from Boroloola:

> That's how at six at night on 11 May 1928 I stopped being a Yanyuwa child and became a nowhere person . . . Motherless, cultureless and stuck in a government institution, not because I'd done anything bad or had been neglected, but because my mother was Aboriginal and my father was not. I ceased to be Aboriginal but would never be white. I was now something bad, shameful, called a half-caste.[33]

This discussion of the problems of passing and of identity returns us to the explanation of family origins that was the subject of an earlier chapter. While Australia was coming to terms with the themes powerfully articulated in the *Bringing Them Home* report, members of my family were involved in our own journey of exploration.

Family Secrets –

Research and Revelation

Throughout my family's exploration of our origins, my sister Mary proved to be a productive researcher, tracking down almost forgotten, long out-of-touch relatives as well as elderly men and women who remembered my father. What surprised us most was that one of our distant cousins said that she had always believed Dad's mother was an Aboriginal woman and that this was a common view among the other branches of the Rule family. Mary then met by chance an elderly woman who we both remembered from childhood. When asked about the matter, she reported that Edith Rule always said that John's mother was a gypsy. Edith was so insistent and repeated the story so often that everyone assumed the truth was that she was a coloured woman and probably part-Aboriginal. Several other informants mentioned that John was known by some of his contemporaries as 'Sambo'. I have no idea if he knew of this or if he was called Sambo to his face. I'm sure he would have been devastated if this was so – the hint of racial derision was too clear.

But the most dramatic information came from a professional

genealogist who carried out an exhaustive research project on our behalf. She quickly turned up my father's birth certificate and his parents' wedding certificate. These both provided useful leads – especially the names of my grandmother's parents on the wedding certificate. But there was not much beyond the names; both were deceased. Margaret Dawson declared on the certificate that she didn't know what her father's occupation had been or where she was born. The most frustrating thing was that neither of Margaret's parents could be found anywhere in the records – there were no relevant birth, death or wedding certificates for those names. Despite the thorough research that followed, our great-grandparents remained little more than names to which no personal history could be attached. Why this was so is hard to determine. Perhaps they had both been born, officially unnoticed, in the bush and had never actually married. But why were there no death certificates? We then wondered if our grandmother had deliberately provided misleading information on her wedding certificate. Did she want to prevent others from finding out where she had come from? When she married she was only nineteen and a ward of the state, the certificate stated, so she may have been an orphan for some time. Perhaps in the name of assimilation she had been taken from her parents and only knew their names. But all attempts to find reference to Margaret in any state or church records proved fruitless.

However, we managed to find out much more about Margaret's life after her marriage. She lived until 1949 – until my father was forty-eight and I was ten. She had three other children after Dad. John's brother Rawdon was born in 1904, and two half-sisters Jessie and Ena in 1916 and 1921 respectively. Margaret married again in 1917 but her second husband died in 1927. Neither Rawdon nor Jessie married but

Ena had a daughter called Caroline, who we traced to Yamba in northern New South Wales.

The discovery of a whole unsuspected branch of the extended family came as a complete surprise and once we had made contact with our cousin Caroline we found out much more. She provided us with numerous new pieces for our jigsaw and we for hers. Margaret Dawson had lived in Newcastle close to her children until the end of her life, although Caroline was quite young when our grandmother died and couldn't remember much about her. By now Aunt Ena and Uncle Rawdon were also dead. Caroline was emphatic that there had never been any mention of indigenous ancestry among her family but she had often been mistaken for an Aborigine. But both Caroline and her father felt that hidden Aboriginality would help explain much about Margaret.

It emerged that Caroline's side of the family knew about Margaret's first child and their understanding was that she had decided to take John to Hobart to live with his father's relatives because she didn't want to have to cope with him in the early years of her marriage. Then, once Rawdon had arrived, they couldn't afford to keep two children. As far as Caroline knew, my father had never made contact with her family. However, things may have been different on their part – Caroline remembered her mother telling a neighbour that Rawdon had been on holiday in Tasmania and had set out to look his brother up. He had actually gone to our house but lost his nerve at the last minute and turned away unseen. But I have a half-memory – no more that an irritating intimation – that the story was slightly different. I think that one night someone knocked on our front door and my father spoke briefly to a visitor. Subsequently I'm sure my mother said my father was outraged that a complete stranger – an impostor – had claimed to be his brother. Whatever version is correct, it's a sad story. The brothers, who looked alike, as we discovered from photographs of Rawdon, either never met or may have done so in a brief moment of high anxiety ending in rebuff for Rawdon and shocked denial by my father.

Since discovering so much more about our family history – and knowing that there is a lot we may never know – I have tried to relate the personal stories of my father and his mother to the broader themes of national history and even to the global story of mixed-race people. In so doing I have also attempted to weave together, however loosely, the various themes of this book.

It seems clear that by the time she met George Rule as a nineteen-year-old, Margaret Dawson had spent at least some time in an institution or a foster home and that she had decided to hide her past. It is just possible that she was one of the first children removed by the New South Wales Protection Board. Hence she provided either incorrect information on her original marriage certificate or incorrect detail on subsequent birth and marriage documents, all of which contain conflicting names and dates. Caroline's father always said that Margaret was very secretive and was a bit of a mystery, although Margaret did claim she was of French extraction, which her family didn't believe for a moment. She never talked about her family at all. They really knew nothing about her past. Caroline remarked that her mother, father and aunt often wondered why Margaret appeared to have no relatives – no brothers, sisters, uncles, aunts or cousins. It was as if she had appeared from nowhere. She apparently had only one relic, which she claimed came from her earlier life. It was a photo of a young girl. But her daughter Ena and grand-daughter Caroline were convinced that it could not possibly be a photo of a younger Margaret. It looked nothing like her.

All this indicates that Margaret had decided to pass into White Australia and leave her past behind. Two things suggest themselves immediately. One is the great, life-distorting handicaps that burdened anyone recognised or identifying as an Aborigine in Australia at the beginning of the twentieth century. There were, to begin with, the legal and institutional barriers; the denial of rights; the vulnerability to official interference. And what could you do when everyone was convinced you were either a Stone-Age primitive or a mixed blood of degenerate character? To be known as a half-caste was to be placed in an encompassing, unbending straightjacket of other people's expectations, to be judged in advance regardless of your individual personality or ability. Margaret's story also indicates what was required in order to blend into society – to move away from where you were known, to invent an ancestry that could explain physical characteristics which differed from those considered typically British, and to make it difficult for anyone to use official documents to track down your past. It was also essential to break away from networks of kin and to never make reference to parents, relatives, birthplace or childhood.

Such passing has probably been quite common in Australian history from the early days of colonisation. It may have been at its height in the early twentieth century as institutional racism clamped down on Aboriginal society. But we know little about it and have no idea of how many individuals and families were involved. It is, however, interesting to consider accounts of similar experiences of black Americans. In his book *New People*, Joel Williams explained that passing meant crossing the race line and winning acceptance as white in a white world. The rate of passing varied 'with the severity of oppression' and was consequently most common in the period 1880 to 1925. The numbers are unknown, but

Williams believed that a conservative estimate was that between 2000–3000 individuals passed every year.

While discussing the process itself, Williams observed that light mulattoes would simply drop out of sight, move to an area where they were not known and 'allow their new neighbours to take them as white'. In the case of darker mulattoes, they passed by moving and taking Spanish, Portuguese or other Latin names in order to explain their distinctive colouring and features. Williams concluded that while passing was relatively easy, the emotional costs were high:

> Not only was there the strain of maintaining the fiction of being white, there was also the necessity of cutting away one's roots. For those who passed permanently it was like a voluntary amnesia in which family and close friends, home and all of the accustomed things of a lifetime were suddenly erased.[1]

My father lived with the consequences of a double passing. His mother left her past behind before he was born and then his Tasmanian relatives in turn made sure he could not subsequently find out anything about her. Margaret Dawson may have deliberately provided little useful information on her wedding certificate; Edith Rule convinced my father that he didn't have a birth certificate at all. His mother and his aunt had both created a double barrier to frustrate any investigation of the past. I have no idea if Dad ever tried to find out about his mother. I often wonder if he asked his Tasmanian relatives about her. I imagine they would have told him that they didn't know who she was or where she came from.

Did this deliberate hiding of the past affect my father's life? That is very hard to determine. Children know so much about their parents, are so familiar with them and yet usually know little of their inner life. My mother was emphatic about the emotional stress John was suffering when she first met him; about his obsession with his lost mother. Whether he continued to carry a residue of this distress is hard to say. He didn't relate easily to people. For that matter, he was never really at ease with his own children. He always seemed to be locked away in his head; both possessor and prisoner of a powerful intellect. But how can one determine whether these characteristics related directly to his peculiar circumstances? One anecdote, however, constantly returns to me. Dad once told my sister Mary, in complete seriousness, that he had never had a dream in his life. This seemed to be a most unusual claim for anyone to make. Was it perhaps an intimation of the emotional consequence of not knowing where he had come from? Had he to be ever on guard, even against his own dreams?

On the other hand, there were obvious benefits for my father that flowed from being taken to live and grow up with his Tasmanian relatives. Margaret Dawson and George Rule lived in poverty. I suspect that George was an alcoholic. I can remember my father saying darkly and enigmatically on numerous occasions that the Rules had a problem with alcohol. I think he was referring to his father. John was far better off in many ways than his younger brother Rawdon. The Tasmanian Rules in the early twentieth century were well-off, well-connected and highly educated for the time. Grandfather Rule had been Director of Education; one uncle was a prominent solicitor; another became the parliamentary draughtsman. On the other side of the family, Rawdon had to leave school early and lacked formal education. But Caroline has told us that he had a restless intellect; he was always talking about ideas and was called 'The Prof' by his workmates because he was always reading.

Sadly, Rawdon died at fifty-six – thirty years before my father. His family were convinced that he suffered lung damage from poor work conditions. In this there were interesting parallels in the careers of the two brothers. Both went to work in the new industrial plants of early twentieth-century Australia – John at the zinc works in Hobart, Rawdon for BHP in Newcastle. John was a qualified industrial chemist, Rawdon a bricklayer. Rawdon worked in the dust-filled coke ovens as they under-went repair; John was a shift boss in the cadmium plant. Neither was a desirable work location. In fact, my father in his early thirties began to show symptoms of cadmium poisoning. The company doctor assured him there was nothing to worry about when he developed ulcers on his legs. But his adoptive father, Henry Reynolds, then Director of the Department of Labour and Industry, took him to a specialist and then insisted that he be transferred from the cadmium plant. Unlike Rawdon, Dad was then able to move out of the metallurgical industry, become a technical adviser to the State government and subsequently gain rapid promotion in the bureaucracy.

So whatever cost my father paid for his separation from his mother, he had a life of extraordinarily diverse achievements. In addition to his two successful sequential careers he was an accomplished writer and historian, producing a notable biography of Edmund Barton in 1948. It was written entirely in his spare time. He was also a major figure in Hobart's intellectual and cultural life for more than fifty years, playing leading roles in groups as diverse as the Philatelic Society, the Fellowship of Writers, the Australian Institute of International Affairs and the Tas-manian Historical Research Association. By any objective measure, my father had a successful life. It's my strong impression that it was also a rich and rewarding one.

Since reading so much of the literature about half-castes, I have often wondered if my parents worried about their children, given the powerful contemporary prejudices against any degree of racial mixture. Considering the secrecy surrounding my father's background and his acute sensitivity about it, the probability is that each would have agonised in isolation. There were strong hints of my mother's anxiety which seem more significant in retrospect. On many occasions when family discussion turned to questions of race or of Aboriginal politics, my mother, almost without fail, would declare that it had been shown there were never any throwbacks when Aborigines mated with Europeans. We found this a gratuitous and mildly eccentric statement because it usually had little to do with the particular subject in hand. We also thought it embarrassing, because she would deliver her manifesto in public and as her sight deteriorated her voice seemed to get louder, so that everyone sitting around us could hear. By the 1980s it seemed like an archaic voice from another era, which of course it was. It was a reminder of how significant the public discussion of the matter had been for her. The biologists were declaring that Aborigines were proto-Caucasians at the precise time that Isabelle was having her first four children, including one who died soon after birth. So her latter-day statements on the matter may have been the only – and inadvertent – intimation she ever allowed us of the pre-natal anxieties she had about how her children would look and how dark they might be.

In Tasmania my father undoubtedly suffered from slights, affronts and insensitivity about his background and his appearance. But race was not a major issue during much of his lifetime. Class was far more significant. His family's social position and status was the most important determinant of his life chances, far outweighing rumours of racial contamination. In fact, he had quite a patrician manner and never suffered fools gladly. He embodied his social position, not his racially mixed origins. For years he was the only Justice of the Peace in our neighbourhood and he took his role seriously and performed it with gravity. He was even sometimes referred to as 'the squire'. I don't think he minded that sobriquet at all.

But I wonder what would have happened to him if he had gone to live in northern Australia as a young man, as I was to do forty years later. In the 1920s, race and caste were the predominating characteristics of society in the north. Colour trumped class every time. Would John have suffered the fate of Norman Shillingsworth, the character in Xavier Herbert's 1938 novel *Capricornia*, who at twenty-two travelled from Melbourne to Darwin? Norman had grown up believing that he was the product of a relationship between his father and a Javanese princess. In Melbourne, Herbert wrote, the people Norman mixed with 'did not bother much about his colour'. But as the ship travelled north his colour became overwhelmingly important. By the time he reached Brisbane he was thought to be Eurasian, and the attitudes of the other passengers changed. Farther north at Port Magnetic (Townsville), he went ashore alone. Several men he tried to befriend in a hotel rebuffed him and one addressed him as a nigger. 'Now he was north of Capricorn', Herbert observed. With the arrival on board of residents returning home to the Northern Territory, Norman's position deteriorated even further. One Territorian said as soon as he set eyes on Norman that he was a 'Yeller Feller' – 'the first he had ever seen aboard a ship, and surely the first that had ever sailed saloon'. From that point on, Norman was totally ostracised.[2]

There are, then, four of us – my sisters Mary and Judy, our cousin Carolyn and myself – the surviving grandchildren of Margaret Dawson.

The discovery of some of the hidden history of our extended family has been the product of an engaging collective enterprise. I think we have all found it to provide unexpected satisfaction. We have discovered things we had not previously thought we needed to know. We have found completeness in places we were unaware of being incomplete.

But what of Aboriginality? It will be clear from the discussion up to this point that the evidence is circumstantial and incomplete. But I think we all agree that this was at the core of the hidden history, the obscured identity. Does this make us Aboriginal? There is no easy answer to that question, nor a collective one. And, what is more, you are damned if you identify and damned if you don't. Such identification has become common, almost fashionable. It should not be lightly undertaken. But avoid identification and others will see it as an exercise in denial, a continuation of an earlier ancestral renunciation. We can be seen, I suppose, as part of what historian Peter Read called 'the lost generations'.

One problem arises from the very effectiveness of Margaret Dawson's passing that means there has not been any public – or, we presume, private – recognition of Aboriginal ancestry in our family for a hundred years. What is more, there seems to be no possibility of returning to any identifiable country, any known community, any rediscovered network of kin. It was a decisive and enduring break. No matter how much we now choose to study anthropology or Aboriginal history, our efforts will still provide us only with understanding and appreciation of things from the outside. Empathy is not the same as identification. And yet I think the four of us welcomed the path along which our suspicions and research led us. I'm not sure that pride is quite the word here. It is not about personal achievement. But I think we have an enhanced sense of belonging to this place – we feel enriched by being able to trace our inheritance back both to the old world and to ancient Australia.

I have Aboriginal friends and acquaintances who have said in the past that they were sure I had some indigenous ancestry. They believed they saw something that I couldn't or wouldn't recognise. My old Guugu Yimidhirr friend Gwen Deemal told me recently that she wasn't at all surprised when I informed her about the book I was writing and the family history we had uncovered. She declared with epigrammatic certainty that the circle was now complete. I had begun my journey when I took up the Aboriginal cause and now I had finally found my way back to my origins. I am never sure how to respond to such suggestions, to the belief that I chose to do my work in Aboriginal history for reasons that were hidden from my conscious mind, that the heart has reasons which reason doesn't know. My sceptical spirit draws me back from such speculation. But I do find it intriguing that my first major book was *The Other Side of the Frontier*, which attempted to relate the history of Australia from an Aboriginal point of view. I am reminded too that my sister Mary began to paint Aboriginal motifs on paper and fabric in her late teens as though it was natural to her. I had discussed in my book *Why Weren't We Told?* the reasons why I had become involved in Aboriginal affairs in north Queensland and then wrote about the history of race relations. On re-reading my own explanation, it seems to remain an adequate account of my political and intellectual development. Many contemporaries pursued the same course. But I'm sure that Gwen Deemal, for instance, will not change her opinion and others may well agree with her.

What our story suggests is the need to accept that many Australians are of mixed ancestry and that elsewhere in the world today we would simply be known and accepted as mestizo. That would seem to be obvious enough, but in Australia the intellectual, political and moral pressure has been to preserve a clear distinction between black and white and to rigorously police the no-man's land between the two camps. As we have seen, these were almost overpowering sentiments forbidding white men to openly acknowledge their Aboriginal sexual partners or their mixed-race children. 'Combos' were social outcasts. Marriage was at an even further remove from acceptable moral terrain. While popular opinion condemned open interracial liaisons, experts lauded White Australia's pride of race. Government policies were grounded in popular opinion. For many years they were premised on the need to separate white and black by establishing closed and isolated Aboriginal reserves, by removing children before they had become attached to their culture, by preventing mixed-race marriages. Differences in living conditions, life chances, political and civil rights were vast and unbridgeable. Australians had to be one or the other, white or black, European or Aboriginal. There was no third option, no intermediate resting point. But there could be movement across the bridge of assimilation. In the past it was often forced and almost always from the black side to the white. In recent times, many of those removed – or their children – have passed back in the other direction. But no one has yet claimed the right to broaden the bridge itself and camp there between the two well-defended positions.

That is where I think we would like to be – to be recognised as belonging to two families at the same time, and not to be forced to choose between them as our grandmother was compelled to do.

I began this book with the observation that my father was a child of the twentieth century. He was born in 1901 and died a few years before the fall of the Berlin Wall. From his early teens until just before his death he took a deep interest in international affairs. He was a witness of the century's terrible calamities, although he was particularly fortunate himself. He was too young for service in World War I and too old for World War II. He was fully employed throughout the Great Depression, and Tasmania was far removed from those places that experienced the century's full horrors. Race thinking bruised him without blighting his life.

Elsewhere, racism was a major factor in many of the century's bitterest tragedies along with the concomitant scourge of exclusive ethnic nationalism. The Armenian genocide and the Holocaust of Jews and gypsies were at the cutting edge of infamy, as was Stalin's ruthless ethnic cleansing. But race also inspired apartheid in South Africa, segregation and lynching in the United States, and the White Australia policy. In the name of eugenics and race betterment, thousands of people were sterilised in American states and European nations. Assimilationist dreams inspired the removal of children from Native American families in the US and gypsy families in Switzerland.

As we have seen, thousands of Aboriginal families were broken up in Australia between 1900 and 1960. Racial categories were used to determine the fate of many children, choosing who would be taken away, how they would be treated and where they were incarcerated. Much of the recent debate about these policies has suffered from a lack of international perspective. One side treats Australia as though it was uniquely racist. The other believes that racism had very little to do with what was a humanitarian project and depicts participants as though they lived in sealed containers of virtue, cut off from the most powerful intellectual currents of the time.

Now, when human biologists tell us that perceived racial characteristics are of minor genetic significance and that there are greater differences within what were once called races than there are between them, it becomes more difficult to understand the dangerous passions that ravaged the world in the twentieth century. But it is something we must never forget. We should remember the 'nowhere people' – the half-castes, the mulattoes and the mestizoes – who were derided and persecuted in many parts of the world, not for what they did or said, thought or believed, but simply for how they looked and what they were.

Notes

Introduction – Mixed Blood

[1] P. Topinard, *Anthropology*, London, 1878, p. 383.

[2] J. Williamson, *New People: Miscegenation and Mulattoes in the United States*, Free Press, New York, 1980, p. 63.

[3] W. E. B. du Bois, 'The Negro Race in the United States of America', in G. Spiller, ed., *Papers on Interracial Problems*, P. S. King, London, 1911, p. 350.

[4] C. White, *An Account of the Regular Gradation in Man*, London, 1799, p. 117.

[5] S. J. Holmes, *The Trend of the Race*, Constable, London, 1921, p. 250.

[6] C. Toibin, 'The Tragedy of Roger Casement', *New York Review of Books*, 27 May 2004, p. 56.

[7] As quoted by S. J. Holmes, *The Trend of the Race*, op. cit., p. 249.

[8] R. R. Rentoul, *Race Culture or Race Suicide*, Walter Scott, London, 1906, p. 4.

[9] W. K. Hancock, *Smuts: The Fields of Force, 1919–50*, Cambridge University Press, Cambridge, 1968, p. 113.

[10] H. H. Johnston, 'Race Problems in the New Africa', *Foreign Affairs*, vol. 2, no. 4, June 1924, pp. 611–12.

[11] J. T. Beckett, 'Chief Protector of Aborigines, Report of Administrator of the Northern Territory, 1914–15', *Commonwealth Parliamentary Papers*, no. 240, 1914–15, p. 27.

[12] 16 August 1928.

[13] Quoted by T. Austin, *I Can Picture the Old Home so Clearly*, Aboriginal Studies Press, Canberra, 1993, p. 55.

[14] D. Bates, *The Native Tribes of Western Australia*, ed. I. White, National Library, Canberra, 1985, p. 311.

[15] *Sunday Times*, 2 October 1921.

Chapter 1 – The Ball and Chain of Hybridism

[1] E. Long, *The History of Jamaica*, 3 vols, London, 1774, II, p. 327.

[2] T. Jefferson, *Notes on the State of Virginia*, Philadelphia, 1788, p. 154.

[3] D. H. Fowler, *Northern Attitudes Towards Interracial Marriage*, Garland Publishing, New York, 1987, pp. 44, 50.

[4] T. Bendyshe, ed., *The Anthropological Treatises of Johann Friedrich Blumenbach*, London, 1865, p. 276.

[5] J. C. Prichard, *The Natural History of Man*, 3rd edn, London, 1848, p. 6.

[6] ibid.

[7] ibid., p. 18.

[8] W. Lawrence, *Lectures on Comparative Anatomy*, 7th edn, London, 1838, pp. 200–3.

[9] Long, op. cit., vol. 2, p. 336.

[10] N. Stepan, *The Idea of Race in Science: Great Britain 1800–1960*, MacMillan, London, 1982, p. 1.

[11] A. de Gobineau, *The Inequality of Human Races* [1854], Heinemann, London, 1915, p. 25.

[12] J. C. Nott & G. R. Gliddon, *Types of Mankind*, Trubner, London 1854, p. 405.

13   J. C. Nott, 'The Negro Race', *Anthropological Review*, vol. 4, July 1866, quoted by J. S. Haller, *Outcasts from Evolution*, McGraw-Hill, New York, 1971, p. 82.

14   R. Knox, *The Races of Men* [1856], 2nd edn, London, 1862, pp. 497, 505.

15   Quoted by L. Menand, *The Metaphysical Club*, Farrar, Straus & Giroux, New York, 2001, pp. 139–40.

16   P. Broca, *On the Phenomena of Hybridity*, London, 1864, pp. 39, 59.

17   G. Pouchet, *The Plurality of the Human Race*, London, 1864, pp. 99, 105–6.

18   N. Stepan, 'Biological Degeneration: Races and Proper Places', in J. E. Chamberlin & Sander L. Gilman, *Degeneration: The Dark Side of Progress*, Columbia University Press, New York, 1985, p. 109.

19   F. Galton, *Inquiries into Human Faculty*, London, 1883, p. 332.

20   Stepan in Chamberlin & Gilman, op. cit., p. 105.

21   H. Spencer, 'Comparative Psychology of Man', *Popular Science Monthly*, January 1876, as quoted by Haller, op. cit., p. 130.

22   Stepan in Chamberlin & Gilman, op. cit., p. 110.

23   C. Darwin, *The Variation of Animals and Plants Under Domestication*, 2 vols, London, 1868, II, p. 47.

24   J. S. Haller, op. cit., pp. 27–9.

25   ibid., p. 160.

26   ibid., pp. 176–7; ibid., p. 65.

27   ibid., p. 65.

28   D. G. Brinton, *Races and Peoples*, New York, 1890, pp. 283–4, 287.

29   E. O. Ross, *Foundations of Sociology*, Macmillan, New York, 1905, p. 379.

Chapter 2 – Fear of Miscegenation

1   Fowler, op. cit., p. 139.

2   ibid., p. 305.

[3] P.S. Reinsch, 'The Negro Race and European Civilisations', *The American Journal of Sociology*, vol. 11, no. 2, September 1905, p. 148.

[4] Seeley Service & Co., London, 1925, pp. 233–4.

[5] 'Proceedings of the American Philosophical Society', vol. 56, 1917, quoted in J.W. Gregory, *Race as a Political Factor*, Watts & Co., London, 1931, p. 43.

[6] G.B. Davenport & M. Steggerda, *Race Crossing in Jamaica*, Carnegie Institute, Washington, 1929, pp. 470–1.

[7] V. MacCaughey, 'Race Mixture in Hawaii', *The Journal of Heredity*, vol. 10, no. 2, Feb. 1919, pp. 94–5.

[8] A.M. Eastabrook & I.E. McDougle, *Mongrel Virginians*, Williams & Williams, Baltimore, 1926, p. 199.

[9] J.A. Mjoen, 'Harmonic and Unharmonic crossings', *The Eugenics Review*, vol. 14, April 1922–March 1923, p. 40. Mjoen quoted by J.W. Gregory in *Race as a Political Factor*, op. cit., p. 48.

[10] S.J. Holmes, *Studies in Evolution and Eugenics*, Routledge, London, 1923, p. 224.

[11] E.M. East, *Mankind at the Crossroads*, Scribners, New York, 1923, p. 127.

[12] W. McDougall, *The Group Mind*, Cambridge University Press, Cambridge, 1920, p. 242.

[13] ibid.

[14] A. Carr-Saunders, *The Population Problem*, Clarendon Press, Oxford, 1922, p. 380.

[15] E. East & D. Jones, *Inbreeding and Outbreeding*, Lippincott, Philadelphia, 1919, pp. 253–55.

[16] S.J. Holmes, *Studies in Evolution and Eugenics*, Routledge, London, 1923, pp. 222–5.

[17] R. Ruggles-Gates, *Heredity in Man*, Constable, London, 1929, pp. 329–30.

[18] A. Keith, *Nationality and Race*, Oxford University Press, Oxford, 1922, p. 380.

[19] W. McDougall, *Ethics and Some Modern World Problems*, Methuen, London, 1924, p. 65.

[20] Carr-Saunders, op. cit., p. 453.

[21] C. C. Brigham, *A Study of American Intelligence*, Princeton University Press, 1925, pp. 205–10.

[22] Carr-Saunders, loc. cit.

[23] East, *Mankind at the Crossroads*, loc. cit.

[24] J. M. Mecklin, *Democracy and Race Fiction*, Macmillan, New York, 1914, p. 154.

[25] E. B. Reuter, *The Mulatto in the United States*, Haskell House, New York, 1918, pp. 205–10.

[26] J. S. Huxley, America Revisited III; The Negro Problem, *The Spectator*, 29 November 1924, p. 821.

[27] G. H. L. F. Pitt-Rivers, *The Clash of Culture and the Contact of Races*, Routledge, London, 1927, p. 28.

[28] L. Darwin, quoted by J. W. Gregory, *The Menace of Colour*, op. cit., p. 232.

[29] E. B. Reuter, *Race Mixture*, McGraw-Hill, New York, 1931, p. 101.

[30] G. Myrdal, *An American Dilemma* [1944] 2nd edn, Harper & Row, New York, 1962, p. 57.

[31] Reuter, *Race Mixture*, op. cit., pp. 82–8.

[32] Myrdal, op. cit., p. 57.

[33] vol. XV, no. 4, January 1910, p. 450.

[34] C. B. Davenport, *Heredity in Relation to Eugenics*, Williams & Norgate, London, 1912, p. 260.

[35] Mecklin, op. cit., p. 143.

[36] ibid., p. 163, Mecklin quoting from 'The West Indian and the American Negro', *North American Review*, vol. CLXXXV, 1907.

[37] ibid., p. 146.

38 ibid., p. 150.

39 ibid., pp. 146–7.

40 Fowler, op. cit., p. 275.

41 Reuter, *Race Mixture*, op. cit., p. 103.

42 E. Westermarck, *The History of Human Marriage*, 3 vols., 5th edn, Macmillan, London, 1921, II, pp. 38, 42.

Chapter 3 – Eugenics – a New Religion

1 F. Galton, *Natural Inheritance*, Macmillan, London, 1889, pp. 2, 197.

2 ibid., p. 9.

3 ibid., p. 11.

4 ibid., p. 198.

5 F. Galton, *Inquiries into Human Faculty*, Macmillan, London, 1883, p. 307.

6 ibid., p. 334.

7 ibid., pp. 1–2.

8 F. Galton, 'Eugenics: Its Definition, Scope and Aims', *Sociological Papers*, Macmillan, London 1905. The lecture was also published in America in *The American Journal of Sociology*, vol. 10, no. 1, July 1904, p. 1.

9 ibid., p. 5.

10 ibid., p. 3.

11 ibid., p. 70.

12 K. Pearson, *The Problem of Practical Eugenics*, Dulau, London 1909, p. 1.

13 K. Pearson, *The Scope and Importance to the State of the Science of Eugenics*, Dulau, London, 1909, p. 10.

14 B. Kidd, *Principles of Western Civilization*, Macmillan, London 1902, pp. 3–6.

15 W. McDougall, *Ethics and Some Modern World Problems*, op. cit., p. 128.

16 J. B. Haycraft, *Darwinism and Race Progress*, London, 1895, p. 10.

[17] B. Kidd, *Social Evolution*, Macmillan, London, 1894, p. 38.

[18] K. Pearson, *National Life from the Standpoint of Science*, A. & C. Black, London, 1901, p. 24.

[19] ibid., p. 41.

[20] Pearson, *The Scope and Importance to the State, etc.*, op. cit., p. 22.

[21] E. G. Conklin, *The Direction of Human Evolution*, Oxford University Press, London, 1922, pp. 45, 53.

[22] E. G. Conklin, *Heredity and Environment in the Development of Men*, Princeton University Press, Princeton, 1915, pp. 484–8.

[23] J. Bryce, 'Relations of History and Geography', *The Contemporary Review*, vol. XLIX, March 1886, p. 442.

[24] J. Bryce, *The Relations Between the Advanced and the Backward Races of Mankind*, Clarendon Press, Oxford, 1902, p. 7.

[25] ibid., pp. 25–6.

[26] ibid., p. 36.

[27] Weatherly, *Race and Marriage*, op. cit., p. 449.

[28] ibid., p. 453.

[29] J. Bryce, 'The Migration of the Races of Man', *Contemporary Review*, vol. LXII, July 1892, p. 149.

[30] C. H. Pearson, *National Life and Character: A Forecast*, Macmillan, London, 1893, p. 84–5.

[31] B. L. Putman Weale, *The Conflict of Colour*, Macmillan, London, 1910, pp. 305–6.

[32] ibid., p. 305.

[33] *American Journal of Sociology*, vol. XIII, March 1908, p. 695.

[34] ibid., vol. XIII, May 1908, pp. 834–5.

[35] A. Keith, *Ethnos, etc.*, Kegan & Paul, London, 1931, p. 7.

[36] Pitt-Rivers, op. cit., p. 27.

[37] Gregory, *The Menace of Colour*, op. cit., p. 11.

[38] L. Stoddard, *The Rising Tide of Colour, etc.*, Chapman & Hall, London, 1920, p. v.

[39] ibid., p. 299.

[40] ibid., p. 298.

[41] ibid., p. 301.

Chapter 4 – The Most Primitive of Man

[1] J. Burnett, *Of the Origin and Progress of Language*, 2nd edn, Edinburgh, 1774, pp. 420–1.

[2] W. Lawrence, *Lectures on Comparative Anatomy Lectures on Comparative Anatomy, etc*, [1819], 9th edn, London 1844, pp. 165–6.

[3] ibid., p. 325.

[4] de Gobineau, op. cit., p. 107.

[5] Prichard, op. cit., p. 236.

[6] C. White, *An Account of the Regular Gradation in Man*, London, 1799, p. 1.

[7] ibid., p. 65.

[8] ibid., p. 67.

[9] ibid., p. 50.

[10] ibid., p. 83.

[11] J. C. Nott & G. R. Gliddon, *Types of Mankind*, London, 1854, p. 450.

[12] ibid., p. 432–3.

[13] G. Combe, *The Constitution of Man*, Edinburgh, 1828, p. 164.

[14] ibid., p. 167.

[15] P. Broca, *On the Phenomena of Hybridity*, London, 1864, p. 45.

[16] Topinard, op. cit. p. 229.

[17] G. Vogt, *Lectures on Man*, London, 1864, p. 92.

[18] T. H. Huxley, *Man's Place in Nature and Other Essays*, Dent, London, 1906, p. 72.

[19] ibid., p. 96.

[20] E. B. Tylor, *Primitive Culture*, 2 vols, [1865], 3rd edn, London 1891, I, p. 32.

[21] ibid., p. 21.

[22] ibid., p. 37.

23 ibid., p. 31.

24 E. B. Tylor, *Anthropology*, [1881], 2nd edn, London, 1892, p. 76.

25 H. Spencer, *The Principles of Psychology*, London, 1855, p. 465.

26 C. Darwin, *The Descent of Man*, [1871], 2nd edn, London, 1874, p. 255.

27 ibid., p. 945.

28 ibid.

29 ibid., p. 241.

30 ibid., p. 297.

31 A. R. Wallace, 'The Action of Natural Selection on Man' in *Half-Hours with Modern Scientists*, 2nd series, New Haven, Connecticut, 1873, p. 21.

32 P. Pulleine & H. Wollard, 'Psychological and Mental Observations on the Australian Aborigines', *Royal Society of South Australia, Proceedings*, vol. 54, 1930, p. 62.

33 East, *Mankind at the Crossroads*, op.cit., p. 274.

34 R. R. Gates, *Heredity and Eugenics*, Constable, London, 1923, p. 225.

35 'Notes on Physical Anthropology of Australian Aborigines and Black–White Hybrids', *American Journal of Physical Anthropology*, vol. 8, no. 1, Jan.–March 1925, p. 87.

36 'The Asymmetrical Character of Human Evolution', *American Journal of Physical Anthropology*, vol. 8, no. 2, April–June 1925, p. 133.

37 E. East, *Biology in Human Affairs*, op. cit., p. 48.

38 ibid., p. 52.

39 F. Galton, *Inquiries into Human Faculty*, op. cit., p. 308.

Chapter 5 – Racial Ideas at the Time of Federation

1 *Commonwealth Parliamentary Debates* (hereafter CPD), vol. 5, 1901, p. 7275.

2 ibid., vol. 4, p. 4804.

3 ibid., vol. 4, p. 4840.

4 ibid., vol. 5, p. 7688.

[5] ibid., vol. 5, p. 6894.

[6] ibid., vol. 4, p. 5770.

[7] ibid., p. 5168.

[8] ibid., p. 4666.

[9] ibid., p. 5922.

[10] ibid., vol. 5, p. 7246.

[11] ibid., vol. 4, pp. 5140–1.

[12] *The Bulletin*, 28 September 1901.

[13] 'A White Australia: What It Means', *The Nineteenth Century*, January, 1904, p. 152.

[14] 'A White or Piebald Australia', *United Australia*, 20 December 1901.

[15] 'The White Race Instinct', *The Bulletin*, 12 July 1902.

[16] *Science of Man*, 22 September 1900, p. 138.

[17] 28 September 1901.

[18] 1 March 1902.

[19] ibid., 16 March 1901.

[20] ibid., 3 May 1902.

[21] CPD, vol. 4, 1901–02, p. 5378.

[22] 16 August, 1899.

[23] *The Bulletin*, 23 February 1902.

[24] J. Fraser, *Husbands: How to Select Them, How to Manage Them, How to Keep Them*, Melbourne, 1900, p. 32.

[25] 16 November 1901.

[26] Watson, 'A White or Piebald Australia', op. cit.

[27] 'Trial of Jimmy Governor', *Sydney Morning Herald*, 23 November 1900.

[28] ibid.

[29] ibid.

[30] ibid.

[31] ibid.

[32] ibid., 24 November 1900.

[33] B. Davies, *The Life of Jimmy Governor*, Ure-Smith, Sydney, 1978, p. 125.

Chapter 6 – A Dying Race

[1] J. Dredge, *Brief Notes on the Aborigines of New South Wales*, Geelong, 1845, p. 9.

[2] Letter from a Gentleman in New South Wales, Methodist Missionary Society Correspondence – In; Australia 1812–26, Folder 4, Australian Joint Copying Programme, FM4, 1398–1421.

[3] As quoted in H. Reynolds, *Frontier*, Allen & Unwin, Sydney, 1987, p. 115.

[4] C. Sturt, *Narrative of an Expedition into Central Australia*, 2 vols, London, 1849, II, p. 277.

[5] *Moreton Bay Courier*, 1 November 1851.

[6] J. L. Stokes, *Discoveries in Australia*, 2 vols, London, 1846, I, p. 89.

[7] Votes and Proceedings of the Legislative Council of Victoria, 1858–9, D.8, pp. 46–8.

[8] J. Bonwick, 'The Australian Natives', *Journal of the Anthropological Institute*, vol. 16, 1887, p. 202.

[9] W. Ramsay-Smith, 'The Place of the Australian Aboriginal in Recent Anthropological Research', *Proceedings Australian Association for the Advancement of Science*, 1908, p. 574.

[10] J. Barnard, 'Aborigines of Tasmania', *Proceedings Australian Association for the Advancement of Science*, vol. 2, 1890, p. 597.

[11] *The Age*, 11 January 1888.

[12] 'Report on the Scientific Expedition to Bellenden Ker Range', *Queensland Votes & Proceedings*, vol. 5, 1889, p. 1213.

[13] *Australian Quarterly*, vol. 1, September 1930, pp. 61–77.

[14] J. Watson Journal, 17 July 1834, Church Missionary Society Papers, C.H./093, Australian Joint Copying Project.

[15] J. Gunther to D. Coates, 12 December 1839, ibid., C.H./047.

[16] Replies to Circular Letters Addressed to the Clergy, *NSW Legislative Council Votes & Proceedings*, 1846, pp. 554, 562, 567.

[17] G. Pouchet, *The Plurality of the Human Race*, Longman, London, 1864, p. 97.

[18] P. Broca, *On the Phenomena of Hybridity in the Genus Homo*, Longman, London, 1864, pp. 48, 59.

[19] A. Keith, *Nationality and Race*, Oxford University Press, Oxford, 1919, p. 14.

[20] J. L. Stokes, *Discoveries in Australia*, 2 vols, London, 1846, vol. 2, pp. 449–53.

[21] Topinard, op. cit., pp. 376–7.

[22] O. Peschel, *The Races of Man*, London, 1876, p. 9.

[23] J. Bonwick, *The Last of the Tasmanians*, London, 1870, pp. 312–13.

[24] E. M. Curr, *The Australian Race*, 4 vols, Melbourne, 1880, vol. 2, p. 264.

[25] E. J. Eyre, *Journals of Expeditions of Discovery in Central Australia, etc.*, 2 vols, London, 1845, II, p. 324.

[26] Melbourne, 1883, p. 252.

[27] Bonwick, op. cit., p. 309.

[28] P. E. de Strezelecki, *Physical Descriptions of New South Wales and Van Diemen's Land*, London, 1846, p. 346.

[29] C. Darwin, *The Descent of Man* [1872], 2nd edn, London, 1883, p. 170.

[30] 'The Growth of a People, etc.', *Records of the Queen Victoria Museum*, no. 1, June 1953, p. 12.

[31] R. Brough-Smyth, *The Aborigines of Victoria*, [1876], 2 vols, Currey, O'Neil, Melbourne, 1972, p. 94.

[32] Curr, *The Australian Race*, vol. 2, Melbourne, 1880, p. 263.

[33] Brough-Smyth, op. cit., pp. 20–21.

[34] Curr, loc. cit.

[35] J. Matthew, *Two Representative Tribes of Queensland*, Fisher Unwin, London, 1910, p. 81.

[36] *Victoria Legislative Council Votes & Proceedings*, 1858–59, as quoted in P. Corris, *Aborigines and Europeans in Western Victoria*, AIASIS, Canberra, 1968, pp. 135–6.

37 *West Australia Votes & Proceedings*, 1874, no. 2, p. 1.

38 Bonwick, op. cit., p. 282.

Chapter 7 – A Problem Emerges

1   L. R. Smith, *The Aboriginal Population of Australia*, ANU Press, Canberra, 1980, pp. 98–9. 'Reports of Board for the Protection of Aborigines', *NSW Votes & Proceedings*, vol. V, 1889; vol. VII, 1890; vol. VII, 1891–2.

2   'Report of the Board for the Protection of Aborigines for 1888', *NSW Votes & Proceedings*, 1889, vol. V.

3   *NSW Parliamentary Debates*, 1887–88, vol. III, p. 5878.

4   ibid., p. 5883.

5   *Bringing Them Home*, Human Rights & Equal Opportunity Commission, Sydney, 1997, pp. 603–4.

6   *NSW Parliamentary Papers*, vol. II, 1920, p. 855.

7   ibid., vol. I, 1921, p. 1015.

8   Quoted by H. Goodall, *Invasion to Embassy*, Allen & Unwin, Sydney, 1996, p. 119.

9   J. Chesterman & B. Galligan, *Citizens Without Rights*, Cambridge University Press, Cambridge, 1997, p. 16.

10 ibid.

11 M. F. Christie, *Aborigines in Colonial Victoria*, Sydney University Press, Sydney, 1979, p. 180.

12 ibid., p. 191.

13 ibid., p. 193.

14 ibid.

15 ibid., pp. 200–1.

16 Chesterman & Galligan, op. cit., p. 21.

17 ibid., p. 26.

18 ibid., p. 24.

19 J. Critchett, *Our Land Till We Die*, Warrnambool Institute Press, Warrnambool, 1980, pp. 50–1.

[20] Chesterman & Galligan, op. cit., p. 29.

[21] L. R. Smith, op. cit., p. 152.

[22] J. Verran in *South Australia Parliamentary Debates*, House of Assembly, 1910, p. 618.

[23] Quoted in C. Mattigley, ed., *Survival in Our Own Land*, Hodder & Stoughton, Sydney, 1988, p. 157.

[24] ibid.

[25] *South Australia Parliamentary Debates*, House of Assembly, 1910, p. 619; Verran quoting W. E. Dalton.

[26] ibid., vol. 1, 1923, p. 709.

[27] ibid., 1910, pp. 1032–3.

[28] *South Australia Parliamentary Debates*, vol. 2, 1921, pp. 1467, 1573.

[29] ibid.

[30] ibid., p. 1574.

[31] ibid., p. 1620.

[32] ibid.

[33] ibid., p. 1469.

[34] ibid., p. 1576.

[35] ibid., vol. 1, 1923, p. 617.

[36] ibid., p. 1016.

[37] 'Royal Commission on the Aborigines', *South Australian Parliamentary Papers*, vol. II, 1913, no. 26, p. ix.

[38] ibid., pp. 7–12.

[39] ibid., p. 125.

Chapter 8 – Outcasts in the Outback

[1] R. L. Jack, *Northmost Australia*, 2 vols, [1922], 1998, Hesperian Press, Perth, II, p. 736.

[2] 61 Vic no. 17.

[3] 'Annual Report of Northern Protector of Aborigines', *Queensland Votes & Proceedings*, vol. II, 1903, p. 461.

[4] 'Annual Report of Chief Protector of Aborigines', *Queensland Votes & Proceedings*, vol. II, 1906, p. 14.

[5] 'Annual Report of Northern Protector of Aborigines', *Queensland Votes & Proceedings*, vol. II, 1903, p. 461.

[6] ibid.

[7] 'Annual Report of Northern Protector of Aborigines', *Queensland Votes & Proceedings*, vol. IV, 1901, p. 133.

[8] ibid., p. 1337.

[9] *South Australian Royal Commission*, 1913, op. cit., p. 112.

[10] 'Annual Report of the Chief Protector for Aborigines', *Queensland Votes & Proceedings*, Second Session, vol. I, 1905, p. 770.

[11] 'Report of Aborigines Department', *Queensland Parliamentary Papers*, vol. 1, 1924, p. 7.

[12] ibid., vol. II, 1920, pp. 232–3.

[13] *Queensland Parliamentary Debates*, vol. CXXXVII, 1921, p. 977.

[14] 'Annual Report of Aborigines Department', *Queensland Parliamentary Papers*, vol. I, 1929, p. 5.

[15] *Queensland Parliamentary Debates*, vol. CLXII, 1932, pp. 1208–11.

[16] *Queensland Parliamentary Papers*, vol. I, 1933, p. 9; vol. I, 1934, p. 9.

[17] 25 GEO.V, no. 38.

[18] *Queensland Parliamentary Debates*, vol. CLXVI, 1934, p. 1687.

[19] 'Annual Report of Aborigines Department', *Queensland Parliamentary Papers*, vol. II, 1937, p. 10.

[20] ibid., vol. II, 1938, pp. 11–12.

[21] *Queensland Parliamentary Debates*, vol. CLXXIV, 1939, p. 458.

[22] ibid., p. 495.

[23] T. Austin, 'a long humiliation': Aboriginal policy in South Australia's Northern Territory, unpublished mss., p. 80.

[24] G. Reid, *A Picnic with the Natives*, Melbourne University Press, 1990, p. 164.

[25] Austin, 'A long humiliation . . .', op. cit., p. 102.

[26] T. Austin, *Simply the Survival of the Fittest*, Historical Society of the Northern Territory, Darwin, 1992, p. 77.

[27] ibid.

[28] *South Australian Parliamentary Papers*, vol. III, 1900, no. 45, p. 13.

[29] Austin, *Simply the Survival . . .*, op. cit., p. 79.

[30] Austin, 'A long humiliation . . .', op. cit., p. 114.

[31] *South Australia Parliamentary Papers*, 1900, op. cit., p. 13.

[32] Basedow recommendations & Spencer's response, in Northern Territory: Aborigines, NAA A1 (A1/15), 1911, 18824.

[33] *South Australia Parliamentary Papers*: House of Assembly, 1910, p. 724.

Chapter 9 – 'Very Immoral Subjects'

[1] University of Queensland Press, St Lucia, 1973, p. 140.

[2] 'Aborigines Department Annual Report', *West Australia Parliamentary Papers*, 1903–4, no. 32, p. 4.

[3] G. Marsden, 'Special Report on Half-Caste Children', 24 October 1896; 'Aboriginal Women and Half-Caste Children', 3 September 1896; West Australia Archives, ACC: 495, Item 35, 49.

[4] 'Annual Report of Aborigines Department', *West Australia Parliamentary Papers*, vol. II, 1901–2, no. 26, pp. 3–4.

[5] ibid., 1902, vol. II, no. 21, p. 3.

[6] ibid., 1901–2, p. 4.

[7] ibid., 1902, p. 3.

[8] Aborigines Department Report, 1901–2, op. cit., p. 50.

[9] ibid., p. 49.

[10] ibid., p. 8.

[11] ibid., 1903–4, op. cit., p. 4.

[12] *West Australia Parliamentary Debates*, v. 25, 1904, p. 663.

[13] Biskup, op. cit., p. 143.

[14] Quoted by S. Stone, ed., *Aborigines in White Australia*, Heinemann, Melbourne, 1974, pp. 129–30.

[15] 'Report of Chief Protector for Aborigines, 1 July 1908–30 June 1909', *Western Australia Votes & Proceedings*, 1909, vol. 2, no. 25, p. 9.

[16] Quoted by C. Choo, *Mission Girls*, University of West Australia Press, Perth, 2001, pp. 148–9.

[17] *West Australia Parliamentary Debates*, vol. 39, 1910–11, p. 1329.

[18] ibid., p. 3191.

[19] Extract reproduced in S. Stone, *Aborigines in White Australia*, op. cit., p. 141.

[20] ibid., pp. 156–9.

[21] Chesterman & Galligan, op. cit., p. 144.

[22] Austin, *I Can Picture the Old Home So Clearly*, op. cit., p. 67.

[23] R. MacDonald, ed., *Between Two Worlds*, IAD Press, Alice Springs, 1995, p. 27.

[24] Austin, *I Can Picture the Old Home So Clearly*, op. cit., p. 58.

[25] 8 Nov. 1924, quoted by Austin, *I Can Picture the Old Home So Clearly*, op. cit., p. 77.

[26] ibid., p. 76.

[27] Quoted in MacDonald, op. cit., p. 25.

Chapter 10 – Breeding Out the Colour

[1] T. Austin, *Never Trust a Government Man: Northern Territory Aboriginal Policy, 1911–1939*, NTU Press, Darwin, 1997, pp. 142–4.

[2] ibid., p. 143.

[3] Cook to Administrator, 31 March 1927, quoted by Austin, op. cit., p. 195.

[4] *Bringing Them Home*, op. cit., p. 645.

[5] Austin, op. cit., p. 195.

[6] *Bringing Them Home*, op. cit., p. 646.

[7] 'Report of Northern Territory for 1937', p. 71; C. E. Cook papers, Northern Territory Archives, NTRS, 281.

[8] 'Report of the Administrator of the Northern Territory, 30 June 1932', *Commonwealth Parliamentary Papers*, vol. 3, 1932–33–34, no.124, p. 8.

9 Cook to Weddell, 23 July 1932, Australian Archives, A1 33/479.

10 'Report of Administrator for Northern Territory, 30 June 1930', *Commonwealth Parliamentary Papers*, vol. IV, 1929–30–31, no. 216, p. 6.

11 Cook to Weddell, 7 Feb. 1933, Australian Archives, AA CRS A659 40/1/403.

12 'Report of Administrator for Northern Territory, 30 June 1932', 'Report of Education Board', p. 14, *Commonwealth Parliamentary Papers*, vol. III, 1932–33–34, no. 124.

13 ibid., p. 15.

14 ibid., 30 June 1937, *Commonwealth Parliamentary Papers*, vol. III, 1937–38–39–40, no. 58, p. 965.

15 Cook to Weddell, 23 July 1932, Australian Archives, A1 33/479; Cook to Weddell, 27 June, ibid., CRS A659, 40/1/408.

16 ibid.

17 Cook to Administrator, 2 Feb. 1932, Australian Archives, A452/54, 1952/414.

18 Cook to Weddell, 27 June 1933, op. cit.

19 ibid.

20 ibid.

21 ibid.

22 ibid.

23 ibid.

24 ibid.

25 Quoted by MacDonald, loc. cit.

26 18 April 1930.

27 ibid.

28 'Report of Protectors Conference', Canberra 1937, op. cit.

29 *West Australia Parliamentary Debates*, vol. 97, 1936, p. 823.

30 W. Ramsay-Smith, 'The Place of the Australian Aboriginal in Recent Anthropological Research', *Report of 11th Meeting AAAS, Adelaide, 1907*, Adelaide, 1908, p. 574.

[31] ibid.

[32] As quoted by R. McGregor, 'An Aboriginal Caucasian: Some uses of racial kinship in early twentieth century Australia', *Australian Aboriginal Studies*, no. 1, 1996, p. 13.

[33] ibid., p. 12.

[34] ibid., pp. 12–13.

[35] See H. Zogbaum, 'Herbert Basedow and the Removal of Aboriginal Children of Mixed Descent from their families', *Australian Historical Studies*, no. 121, April 2003, p. 125.

[36] ibid., p. 129.

[37] ibid., p. 130.

[38] Tebbutt published his results in the *Medical Journal of Australia*. See McGregor, 'An Aboriginal Caucasian', op. cit., p. 13.

[39] 'The Native of Central Australia', *Proceedings of the Royal Geographical Society; South Australian Branch*, vol. XXXV, 1933–34, pp. 69–70.

Chapter 11 – 'A Colossal Menace'

[1] A. Haebich, *For Their Own Good*, University of Western Australia Press, Perth, 1988, p. 315.

[2] W. H. Kitson in *West Australia Parliament Debates*, vol. 83, 1929, p. 1521.

[3] ibid., vol. 97, 1936, p. 822.

[4] ibid., p. 831.

[5] ibid., 1929, p. 1833.

[6] ibid., 1929, p. 1844.

[7] ibid., 1936, p. 831.

[8] *West Australia Votes & Proceedings*, vol. 1, 1935, no. 2, p. 8.

[9] *West Australia Parliamentary Debates*, vol. 97, 1936, p. 822.

[10] ibid., p. 934.

[11] ibid., p. 830.

[12] ibid., p. 823.

[13] ibid., p. 831.

[14] W. J. Mann, ibid., p. 878.

[15] ibid., vol. 83, 1929, p. 2105.

[16] *West Australia Votes & Proceedings*, vol. 2, 1935, no. 22. p. 1.

[17] 'Coloured Folk', *The West Australian*, 18 April 1930.

[18] Quoted by P. Jacobs, *Mister Neville*, Fremantle Arts Centre Press, 1990, p. 221.

[19] Chesterman & Galligan, op. cit., p. 131.

[20] Quoted by P. Jacobs in 'Science and Veiled Assumptions: Miscegenation in W.A. 1930–1937', *Australian Aboriginal Studies*, no. 2, 1986, p. 15.

[21] Jacobs, *Mister Neville*, op. cit., pp. 256–7.

[22] ibid., p. 256.

[23] *Daily News*, 3 Oct. 1932 as quoted by Jacobs, op. cit., p. 195.

[24] *Australia's Coloured Minority: Its Place in the Community*, Currawong Publishing, Sydney, 1944, p. 11.

[25] ibid., pp. 13–14.

[26] ibid., p. 56.

[27] ibid., p. 176.

[28] ibid., p. 177.

[29] ibid., p. 179.

[30] ibid., p. 177.

[31] ibid., p. 180.

[32] Report on conference in Western Australia State Archives, ACC 993, 427/36.

[33] ibid.

[34] ibid.

[35] ibid.

Chapter 12 – The Caste Barrier

[1] Native Welfare Council, 1939, p. 3.

[2] ibid., p. 2.

[3] ibid., p. 6.

[4] ibid., pp. 22–3.

[5] ibid., p. 27.

[6] N. B. Tindale, 'Survey of the Half-Caste Problem in South Australia', *Proceedings of the Royal Geographical Society of Australasia; South Australian Branch*, vol. XLII, 1940–41, p. 160. See also: A. Charlton, 'Colour Counts: Norman Tindale and the Mathematics of Race', in M. Crotty, et al., eds, *A Race for a Place*, University of Newcastle, 2000, pp. 79–84.

[7] ibid., p. 158.

[8] ibid., p. 102.

[9] ibid., p. 67.

[10] ibid., p. 115.

[11] ibid., p. 132.

[12] ibid., p. 67.

[13] ibid., p. 68.

[14] ibid., p. 135.

[15] ibid., p. 142.

[16] 'The Growth of a People . . . etc.', *Records of the Queen Victoria Museum*, no. 1, June 1953, p. 2.

[17] ibid., p. 22. See also N. B. Tindale, *Journal of Harvard and Adelaide Anthropological Expedition*, Museum of South Australia Archives, AA338/1/15/1, p. 137.

[18] M. Reay, 'A Half-Caste Aboriginal Community in North-Western New South Wales', *Oceania*, vol. 15, no. 4, June 1945, pp. 304–5.

[19] M. Reay, 'Colour Prejudice at Collarenebri, NSW' in *The Aborigines Protector*, vol. 2, no. 3, 1947, p. 10.

[20] M. Reay, 'A Half-Caste Aboriginal Community', op. cit., p. 298.

[21] M. J. Calley, 'Race Relations on the North Coast of New South Wales', *Oceania*, vol. xxvii, 1956–7, p. 196.

[22] ibid., p. 201.

23 C. Kelly, 'The Reaction of White Groups in Country Towns of New South Wales to Aborigines', *Social Horizons*, July 1943, p. 37.

24 R. A. Fink, 'The Caste Barrier – An Obstacle to the Assimilation of Part-Aborigines in North-West New South Wales', *Oceania*, vol. xxviii, no. 2, December 1957, pp. 100–1.

25 M. Reay, 'Colour Prejudice at Collarenebri, NSW', loc. cit.

26 ibid., p. 13.

27 Tindale, 'Survey of the Half-Caste Problem in South Australia', loc. cit. See also: A. Charlton, 'Colour Counts: Norman Tindale and the Mathematics of Race', in M. Crotty, et al., eds, *A Race for a Place*, University of Newcastle, 2000, pp. 79–84.

28 *South Australian Royal Commission*, op. cit., p. 18.

29 ibid., p. 52.

30 ibid., p. 55.

31 ibid., pp. 70–2.

32 ibid., p. 58.

33 Tindale, 'Survey of the Half-Caste Problem in South Australia', loc. cit. See also: Charlton, loc. cit.

34 'The Half-Caste in Australia', *Mankind*, vol. iv, no. 7, September 1951, p. 287.

35 A. O. Neville, *Australia's Coloured Minority*, Currawong Publishing, Sydney, 1947, p. 14.

36 ibid., p. 22.

37 ibid., p. 22.

Chapter 13 – Removing Children

1 CPD, vol. 208, June 1950, p. 3977.

2 'The Future of the Australian Aborigines', Hasluck Papers, ANL No. 5274/38.

3 CPD, vol. 214, 18 October 1951, p. 875.

4 Hasluck Papers, op. cit., Box 38.

[5] J. P. M. Long, 'The Administration of the Part-Aboriginals of the Northern Territory', *Oceania*, vol. XXXVII, no. 3, March 1967, p. 196.

[6] J. C. Archer, Dept. of Territories to F. H. Rowe, Dept. of Social Services, 16 February 1956, NAA, A884/7, A650 Part 1.

[7] C. R. Lambert, Dept. of Territories to Director General, Dept. of Social Services, Melbourne, 1 October 1952, op. cit.

[8] Quoted by J. O'Laughlin in Cubillo & Gunner v Commonwealth of Australia, 2000 *FCA* 1084, pp. 101–2.

[9] As cited by A. Haebich, *Broken Circles*, Fremantle Art Centre Press, 2000, p. 282. See also *Rene Baker*, Fremantle Art Centre Press, forthcoming, p. 61.

[10] ibid., p. 283.

[11] ibid., p. 281.

[12] C. Sturt, *Narrative of an Expedition into Central Australia*, 2 vols, London, 1849, II, p. 285.

[13] Neville, op. cit., pp. 177–80.

[14] R. Manne, 'In Denial', *Australian Quarterly Essay*, no. 1, 2001, pp. 24–8.

[15] P. Read, *A Rape of the Soul So Profound*, Allen & Unwin, Sydney, 1999, pp. 26–7.

[16] *Bringing Them Home*, Human Rights & Equal Opportunity Commission, Sydney, 1997.

[17] See for instance: *C. Mattingley & K. Hampton, eds, *Survival in Our Own Land*, Hodder & Stoughton, Sydney, 1988.
   * *Telling Our Story*, Aboriginal Legal Service, Western Australia, Perth, 1995.
   * D. Mellor & A. Haebich, eds, *Many Voices*, National Library, Canberra, 2002.
   * C. Bird, ed., *The Stolen Children: Their Stories*, Random House, Sydney, 1998.

[18] See for instance: *Read, op. cit.
   * R. Manne, 'In Denial', op. cit.

* Haebich, *Broken Circles*, op. cit.

* Bird, op. cit.

19 See for instance: H. J. Muir, *Very Big Journey*, Aboriginal Studies Press, Canberra, 2004; C. Smith, *Country, Kin and Culture*, Wakefield Press, Adelaide 2004.

20 R. Wilson, Preface in C. Bird, op. cit., pp. xiv.

21 C. Smith, op. cit., pp. 88–9.

22 B. Clarke, *Wisdom Man*, Penguin, Melbourne, 2005, p. 141.

23 Evidence of Bobby Brown in Mellor & Haebich, p. 57.

24 Mellor & Haebich, op. cit., p. 30.

25 ibid.

26 ibid., p. 63.

27 *Bringing Them Home*, op. cit., p. 185.

28 Bird, op. cit., p. 22.

29 Mellor & Haebich, op. cit., p. 61.

30 C. Smith, op. cit., p. 78.

31 ibid., p. 118.

32 ibid.

33 Muir, op. cit., p. 43.

Postscript – Family Secrets – Research and Revelation

1 J. Williams, *New People*, Free Press, New York, 1980, pp. 100–3.

2 X. Herbert, *Capricornia*, (1938), 3rd edn, Angus & Robertson, Sydney, 1956, pp. 181, 186–7.

Further Reading

There is a vast literature about racial ideas, and more specifically about miscegenation. Much of it is hard to access. Fortunately, there are many relevant books that have been published during the last forty or fifty years that should be readily available. The best place to begin is with the general surveys of the history of racial ideas. See for instance:

Fredrickson, C. M., *The Black Image in the White Mind*, Harper-Row, New York, 1971.

——, *Racism: A Short History*, Scribe, Melbourne, 2002.

Hannaford, I., *Race: The History of an Idea in the West*, The Woodrow Wilson Press, Washington, 1996.

Snyder, L. L., *The Idea of Racialism: Its Meaning and History*, Van Hostrand, Princeton, 1962.

For works that focus on science and race, refer to:

Haller, J. S., *Outcasts from Evolution: Scientific Attitudes of Racial Inferiority 1859–1900*, McGraw Hill, New York, 1975.

Stepan, H., *The Idea of Race in Science: Great Britain 1860–1960*, Macmillan, London, 1982.

For the specific questions of intermarriage and miscegenation consult:

Fowler, D. H., *Northern Attitudes Towards Interracial Marriage*, Garland Publishing, New York, 1987.

Henriques, F., *Children of Caliban: Miscegenation*, Secker & Werbury, London, 1974.

Williamson, J., *New People: Miscegenation and Mulattoes in the United States*, The Free Press, New York, 1980.

For the systematic attack on race thinking after World War II see Kuper, L., ed., *Race, Science and Society*, Allen & Unwin, London, 1975.

Among the array of relevant publications the following will be found useful:

Call, J. W., *The Highest Stage of White Supremacy: The Origins of Segregation in South Africa and the American South*, Cambridge University Press, Cambridge, 1982.

Chamberlain, J. E. & S.L., eds, *Degeneration: The Dark Side of Human Progress*, Columbia University Press, New York, 1985.

Ernst W., & Harris, B., eds, *Race, Science and Medicine, 1700–1960*, Routledge, London, 1999.

Knight, D., *Ordering the World: A History of Classifying Man*, Burnett Books, London, 1981.

Lorimer, D. A., *Colour, Class and the Victorians*, Leicester University Press, Leicester, 1978.

Numbeas, R. L. & Stenhouse, J., eds, *Disseminating Darwin: The Role of Place, Race, Religion and Gender*, Cambridge University Press, Cambridge, 1999.

Stepan, N. L., *'The Hour of Eugenics': Race, Gender and Nation in Latin America*, Cornell University Press, Ithaca, 1991.

There has been considerable discussion in Australia about racial ideas but not all that much about the cultural themes of this book. However, in the last few years a number of excellent studies have appeared. See for instance:

Anderson, W., *The Cultivation of Whiteness: Science, Health and Racial Destiny in Australia*, Melbourne University Press, Melbourne, 2002.

Briscoe, G., *Counting, Health and Identity: A History of Aboriginal Health and Demography in Western Australia and Queensland, 1900–1940*, Aboriginal Studies Press, Canberra, 2003.

McGregor, R., *Imagined Destinies: Aboriginal Australians and the Doomed Race Theory, 1880–1939*, Melbourne University Press, Melbourne 1997.

Each book has an extensive bibliography containing many leads to a large amount of relevant literature. There is also considerable literature about mixed-descent, fringe-dwelling communities. Some of it is not easily accessible. The classic summary of much of the post-World War II research will be found in: Rowly, C. D., *Outcasts in White Australia*, [1972], Penguin Books, Ringwood, 1973.

For a more recent study of fringe-dwelling communities, consult Haebich, A., *For Their Own Good: Aborigines and Government in the South West of Western Australia, 1900–1949*, 3rd edn, University of Western Australia Press, Nedlands, 1998.

Another useful volume about racial policies is the study of A. O Neville: Jacobs, P., *Mister Neville*, Fremantle Arts Centre Press, Fremantle, 1990.

The discussion during the 1990s about reconciliation and the stolen generation has resulted in a number of relevant books. The starting point must be the report of the Human Rights & Equal Opportunity Commission on the stolen children: *Bringing them Home: National Inquiry into the Separation of Aboriginal and Torres Strait Islander Children from Their Families*, Human Rights & Equal Opportunity Commission, Sydney, 1997. But see also:

Bird, C., ed., *The Stolen Children: Their Stories*, Random House, Sydney, 1998.

Haebich, A., *Broken Circles*, Fremantle Arts Centre Press, 2000.

Manne, R., 'In Denial: the stolen generation and the Right', *Australian Quarterly Essay*, no. 1, 2001.

Mellor D. & Haebich, A., eds, *Many Voices*, National Library, Canberra, 2002.

Read, P., *A Rape of the Soul So Profound*, Allen & Unwin, Sydney, 1999.

Aboriginal history, either as oral history collections or autobiography and memoir, contains much graphic evidence. See for instance:

Clarke, B., *Wisdom Man*, Penguin, Melbourne, 2005.

Mattingley, C. & Hampton, K., eds, *Survival in Our Own Land*, Hodder & Stoughton, Sydney, 1988.

Muir, H. J., *Very Big Journey*, Aboriginal Studies Press, Canberra, 2004.

Powell, R. & Kennedy, B., *Rene Baker, File # 28/EDP*, Fremantle Arts Centre Press, Fremantle, 2005.

Smith, C., *Country, Kin and Culture*, Wakefield Press, Adelaide, 2004.

Telling Our Story, Aboriginal Legal Service, Western Australia, Perth, 1995.

Index

ALSO BY HENRY REYNOLDS

WHY WEREN'T WE TOLD?

Why were we never told? Why didn't we know?

Historian Henry Reynolds has found himself being asked these questions by many people, over many years, in all parts of Australia. The acclaimed *Why Weren't We Told?* is a frank account of his personal journey towards the realisation that he, like generations of Australians, grew up with a distorted and idealised version of the past. From the author's unforgettable encounter in a North Queensland jail with injustice towards Aboriginal children, to his friendship with Eddie Mabo, to his shattering of the myths about our 'peaceful' history, this bestselling book will shock, move and intrigue. *Why Weren't We Told?* is crucial reading on the most important debate in Australia as we enter the twenty-first century.

'This is a fine and engaging memoir. It is also a fascinating book about the writing of history, by one of its master practitioners in this country.'
Michael Duffy, *The Australian*

'*Why Weren't We Told?* urges us to continue to search for the truth about our past in order to prepare for and safeguard our future.'
Andrea Durbach, *The Bulletin*

'A must-read ... I found the story of Reynolds' intellectual and spiritual journey moving and thought-provoking.'
Noel Pearson, *The Age*